Wallace

GW01458459

Of Pedigree Unknown

sporting and working dogs
Of Pedigree Unknown

PHIL DRABBLE

London
Michael Joseph

First published in Great Britain by Cassell & Co 1964
This edition published by Michael Joseph Ltd
52 Bedford Square, London, W.C.1
1976

© 1964 and 1976 by Phil Drabble

ISBN 0 7181 1447 7

Printed in Great Britain by
Hollen Street Press Ltd at Slough
and bound by James Burn at Esher, Surrey

To those who like their dogs for the companionship
they bring, and care little for the fictitious values long
pedigrees sometimes bestow

Contents

Illustrations

All photographs are by Derek Johnson

Preface

My dogs earn their place on the hearth by deeds not looks. If they are faithful, hardy and intelligent, I don't care a jot if their pedigrees are wrapped in mystery.

For more than twenty years my hobby was ratting and I believe that rats are the slickest, most cunning quarry that I ever pitted my wits against. Men who could think and act as quickly in tight corners would soon be tycoons.

I am glad that the 1973 Badgers Act has made badger digging illegal because I am particularly fond of badgers and digging them with terriers was often exceptionally cruel to both dog and quarry. Competitive hare coursing is out of favour though the act appears to have been drafted largely to prevent competitive coursing meetings and there will still be nothing to stop a loose dog giving chase to a hare which "happens" to get up in front of him. Long dogs and their owners may still be able to catch their dinner without penalty—unless they are poaching.

Whippet racing is now more popular than at any time since the Great War and no sport is more spectacular. Rabbits are holding their own with myxomatosis and the most scientific Pest Destruction Officer does no better than old-fashioned rat catchers, so that there is as yet no prospect that quarry will run out for sporting dogs.

P.D.   September 1975

1. First Love

Nothing spoils dogs like shows. Scientific breeders have exaggerated superficial appearance, often at the expense of stamina and courage and brains, until many modern show-dogs are but miserable caricatures of the original animals which made their breed famous. The asthmatic wheezing of a show bulldog, born by Caesarean operation because his mother was too deformed to deliver him naturally, is an eloquent protest against dog-fanciers who have ruined an agile breed for money.

Fashion is as fickle and illogical with breeds of dogs as it is with ladies' hats. But if one has no background oneself, it has become almost a social necessity to own a dog, almost any dog, so long as his claims to nobility are documented by a pedigree with a champion in almost every line. So long as the price is obviously prodigious, it does not seem to matter if the dog is physically unsound or mentally insane.

When I grew up between the wars, before the affluent days when status symbols mattered, we liked our dogs to be useful more than ornamental. Indeed many people preferred mongrels to showdogs 'because they were so much more intelligent'.

Mick was my first and one of my best-loved dogs. He was

with me, as constantly as school would allow, from when I was eight until he died, when I was nineteen. He wouldn't have been rated very highly in the modern social scale. His mother was a working fox terrier, small enough to go to ground and bolt a fox, agile enough to keep up, all day, with hounds and strong enough to kill rats as quickly as they could be persuaded by ferrets to leave their holes. She was first owned by a little girl, less precocious in her grasp of the facts of life than is now the fashion, who had named her Peter. And Peter she was called for the rest of her life. She was a gentle soul who must always have pined for the petting of her first young owner, and it was not until the ferret box was unhooked from the nail on the pigsty wall that she really came alive. Then her feet never seemed to touch the ground simultaneously, so incessant was her war-dance; her eyes shone as if she had swallowed a packet of pep-pills and she whimpered a continuous high-pitched war-cry. Although she was as game as a fighting cock and would bolt a fox or kill a rat with the best, she really shone at rabbiting. She knew exactly how important silence was; her whimpering soliloquy ceased and she trod suddenly silent as a cat. She would sniff the mouth of a hole as delicately as a connoisseur savouring the bouquet of his brandy, and it was obvious at a glance if there was anything at home. If she passed sedately on, it was a waste of time putting a ferret down the hole, but if there was a rabbit there, her tail would quiver and her whole body go tense with excitement as she crouched in anticipation. Nets would be put over the holes and a ferret quietly popped into a likely entrance.

During the silence which followed, her infectious excitement would grip us too, so that if a rabbit did explode into a net, the surprise always made me jump, although I could gauge exactly when it was coming by watching the quivering expectancy of the dog freeze, for the last split second, into immobility.

Occasionally the bury, or warren, would be exceptionally

2

large or the cover so thick that it was impossible to pop a purse net over every hole. Then it nearly always happened that the rabbits would pick as their escape the very holes we had missed. Peter seemed gifted with second sight. She was far too small to have the least chance of catching a rabbit by coursing it in the open. Her great ears were very large for her head and always pricked, and they would flex and turn as she located the rumblings below ground, so that she was always a move ahead and in exactly the right position to cut off the bolting rabbit's escape. A neat dive, like the tackle of a rugby full-back, a flurry of white and brown, a piercing scream as the rabbit felt the teeth of doom, and she was ready for the next. How she killed them so quickly, when she was so slightly bigger or stronger, puzzles me now, though I took it for granted in my childhood inexperience.

If, as often happened, the rabbit decided that the devil he knew, in ferret form, was preferable to the devils he didn't know, consisting of Peter and us, then he wouldn't bolt. Instead he stayed below ground, his head jammed tight up the dead-end of a burrow with his backside filling the tunnel, like a woman with the middle-age spread. The purpose was to prevent the ferret clambering over his body to sink deadly teeth in his neck or in his spine where it joined the skull. All the frustrated ferret could do was to scratch and gnaw ineffectually at her quarry's haunches in the hope of being able to inch over to somewhere more vital.

From our point of view it was often a cold and always a rather boring interlude. There was nothing to see and nothing to hear. A line ferret was sent down to find his mate and dislodge or kill her quarry. Knots in the line at yard intervals indicated how far the liner had gone in his subterranean meanderings, but since he might have turned many corners, there was little factual indication where he was when he found his mate and her quarry. Or there would have been little indication if it hadn't been for Peter.

She would creep stealthily to the nearest hole, her great

3

prick-ears distilling and locating every sound from below. Occasionally there would be a rumble as the rabbit's thumping feet kicked out at the ferrets or he moved to an even more inaccessible pipe, and the terrier would use every sound to locate the quarry, until at last she would sit crouched and expectant exactly above them. All that was now necessary was to dig gently down with a spade until the ground crowned in and ferrets and rabbit could be lifted out by hand. Without a dog, it would have been necessary to dig a trench, or, at best, a whole series of holes, to follow the course of the line ferret's wanderings by tracing the line he had dragged through the tunnels.

Peter saved an immense amount of work and time out rabbiting, but she could have done with just a little more toughness and dash for ratting, and so she was mated to a Staffordshire Bull Terrier.

Some people would have called the resulting puppies mongrels. They were certainly cross-breds, but it was a deliberate cross aimed to combine the qualities of both bull and fox terriers, and was by no means the street accident that conceives mongrels in the derogatory sense.

Although the puppies were 'of pedigree unknown', any virtues they possessed were due more to judgement than luck. Certainly the pup that came to us had all the qualities a dog should have.

He was my eighth birthday present and ten bob was never better spent. It took a little time for his attractions to become obvious to my mother, who only saw an ugly smooth-haired pup, white with lemon on his head, pot-bellied with worms, shrill-voiced with complaint at being taken too soon from his mother, and fuller than a well with water—if puddles he left on the carpet were any criterion.

But to me he had promise which was fulfilled tenfold in the future.

We had never had a dog at home before and knew nothing of house training or, indeed, training of any sort. Mick was

4

short-haired and felt the cold, his worms made him eat pro-
digiously to satisfy their appetite, and he was so eager to please
that the least scolding hurt his feelings and made him cringe
as if he had been whipped. He would have been a difficult
proposition for anyone with the advantage of an intelligent basic knowledge of how to handle dogs. To us, the
task was impossible. The result was that he wasn't clean in the
house until he was more than six months old. Six months
during which we learnt far more than he did, though the
knowledge we gained was largely at his expense. The man who
sold him to us thought he 'might have a worm or two'. So
he thrust down his throat a cud of twist tobacco, which got
rid of the worms in a writhing, evil-smelling mass as big as
a tennis-ball, but made his young stomach so intolerant of
food for so long that he nearly died. He told us that if he
made a mess in the house we should rub his nose in it and give
him a good hiding; instead we should simply have put him
out of doors, after meals and sleep, until he emptied himself,
so that being clean would quickly have been a reflex. Good
hidings and long periods of banishment merely made him so
sensitive that he would suddenly take fright for no apparent
reason and yell his head off as if demons were knocking hell
out of him, despite the fact that he was never hit by anything
more painful than a rolled-up newspaper, which rattled but
did not hurt.

Mick developed into a wonderful dog, in spite of the
stupidity of his owners. When he was seven months old I
took him shopping on his lead, tripped over a paving-stone
and cut my knee so badly that I couldn't get up. I lay and
howled as most eight-year-olds would, and was soon surrounded by sympathizers ready and willing to take me home.
But no one could touch me. My timid pup was suddenly a
fury standing guard ready to tear to shreds the first person to
touch me. His backside took after Peter, his mother, and was
typical of a smallish fox terrier. Just as the best athletes are
often slim-waisted, spreading to powerful chests and shoulders,

the front end of Mick was in best bull terrier tradition. So was his head, which was broad and strong with the friend-liest grin when all was well; but he had a jaw like an alligator when he meant business.

He certainly meant business as he stood guard over my prostrate, blarting form, and it was some time before a helper had the wit to instruct me to tie his lead to a railing and crawl out of reach. I shall never forget the paroxysms of his fury when he discovered he could not get near enough to defend me and I was carried away by strangers. Nor shall I forget the joy of reunion when my father collected him after binding up my knee.

That episode was the turning-point in Mick's career. Until then he had been regarded by the family as an unmitigated nuisance, yapping by day and wetting the carpet at night. He had lived under a constant threat of return to the man who had sold him, and I had been his only ally. Suddenly it was realized that he was a redoubtable bodyguard, whose courage was to be admired all the more because he was by nature no aggressive fool but extremely sensitive and kind.

His sporting career started shortly afterwards. I had seen his previous owner rabbiting with ferrets and I decided my life would be incomplete without a ferret of my own. I drew a blank with Peter's owner, who had now given up ferrets in favour of racing pigeons, and I was introduced to the head keeper of the local estate who found he could 'spare' me a young ferret for seven and sixpence. That was a very high price for a ferret before the war, and I have since realized that keepers cannot often meet fools or children with whom to trade so profitably. In any case, I have since been extremely wary of keepers' ferrets, because I find few keepers bother to handle them enough to get them properly tame. This first ferret that I bought was one of a litter in a hutch, and on the roof of the hutch was a dead rabbit. The standard method of catching a youngster was to dangle the rabbit in the hutch so that all the ferrets caught hold, and then throttle one of them

6

off, so that he was already held safely by the neck before his teeth were disengaged from the rabbit.

I took it home in innocent pride, having been milked of my seven and sixpence, and put it in the box I had prepared. Within ten minutes my patience at being parted was exhausted; I opened the lid and put my hand in, full of confidence because the keeper had told me how quiet they all were. The ferret, seeing something approach, advanced in the expectation of another helping of rabbit, and took a firm hold of my thumb. I had never had proper lessons on how to choke a ferret off, nor how to pinch his foot to make him leave go, nor even how to bite his tail. So the ferret hung on and shook like a fox terrier, in the hope that a piece of flesh small enough to swallow would tear away.

It was not the ideal introduction to ferrets for a child of eight, and it put me off ferrets entirely until the next holiday. The only consolation was that my father was so incensed that, when the ferret did let go, he popped a bucket over it—not wishing to get bitten by picking it up himself—put a brick on the bucket and went to fetch the keeper who had sold it to me as 'quiet'. I felt a little mollified when he was bullied into disgorging my seven and sixpence and then left to walk back home three miles on a wet Sunday night. By next holidays I had forgotten the pain and longed to go ferreting myself. In those days the standard way of 'breaking a dog in to rats' was to buy a live rat from the local ratcatcher and introduce it to the dog. One or other was bound to come off best, and it was said that no dog would become a good ratter until he had been bitten.

This would be strictly illegal nowadays, as any R.S.P.C.A. man would regard releasing a captive rat to a dog as 'baiting'. Indeed, it was illegal even in my young day, but everyone said that 'it was only a rat' and 'didn't matter'. It was considered quite all right to kill rats by any means, few people objected to hunting—because foxes were 'nasty' too—but there was already slight antipathy to stag hunting, 'because

7

deer are such noble beasts'. There has never been much logic where passions of the chase are aroused, whether one loves hunting or would try to prevent it.

At the age of eight, such arguments passed over my head. All I wanted was a ferret of my own and to train my dog to work well with it. Neither was very difficult. Our local rat-catcher was a man called Kelly, who lived in the next village. He was small and sallow, with brown eyes and a sandy moustache and hair. Since a great deal of his time was spent lying full-length on the ground, an ear to a hole listening for sounds of battle below, or with an arm stretched full-length as he reached for his ferret, his clothes were sandy-coloured too. I have often thought since that, if he crouched full-length on a bed of autumn leaves, his camouflage would have been so perfect that he would have been invisible to the most observant eye.

The one thing that betrayed his presence from afar was an overpowering smell of haddock. He was a bachelor and lived alone, so I suppose nobody minded, and his quarry, the rats, may well have found his bouquet dangerously seductive. Perhaps the Pied Piper of Hamelin exercised a similar charm over the rats of that city.

The first time I met him, being a polite child, I called him Mr Kelly. It was a title he must have found strange, for his betters called him Kelly and his equals 'Hairy Kelly' or just 'Hairy', depending on how well they knew him.

The impact of my first courtesy made such an impression on him that he sold me a jill ferret for three and sixpence, which was a considerable improvement on the keeper's price. And he told me that, though he did sell rats to people who wanted to break a dog in, he would not advise me to introduce Mick in cold blood. The first thing, he said, was to get him safe to ferrets, and only then to let him meet a rat in hot blood; so I took Mick and my ferret away and spent the next week first holding the ferret and letting him smell it, then holding him on a lead while the ferret ran round and, finally,

8

allowing them both to be loose together. Then I returned, demonstrated my success at this first attempt at dog training, and was invited out for half a day's ratting.

It was the most exciting day I had ever had in my life: formalities were dropped, 'Mister' gave way to the ubiquitous 'Hairy', and I became 'Oi, kid' instead of 'Master Phil'. It was one of those golden days at the end of the summer holidays which made the prospect of stuffy schoolmasters and hearty boys bent on rugger and other mass activity unthinkable. The corn was cut and rats which had lived in the secluded security of a hedge between two cornfields were suddenly exposed to danger. There was no doubt where they lived; piles of ears of wheat, the grain eaten or wastefully scattered, were clear enough evidence of the presence of thieves: runs, padded bare along the bottom of the hedge, showed the paths they took between the comfort of the warren and drinking places, where water lay in the bottom of the ditch. Hairy did his detective work aloud—'A cobweb on this hole, so they aren't in here.' 'Grass growing in the mouth of that, so they've left there.' Gradually he pieced the evidence together and deduced that the whole colony had settled at one end of the hedge in a large bank of soil in the corner of the field. His soliloquy and any conversation between us was carried on in conspiratorial whispers, and I was gratified to discover that he liked me because I was 'a quiet kid': he 'couldn't abear', it seemed, 'babblers'.

I kept Mick on his lead, so that he didn't betray his presence by blowing his excitement down the holes. Hairy's little dog, sandy and unkempt like himself, kept strictly at his heels where experience had taught him that he was least likely to get a kick in the ribs. I discovered later that, although Hairy did use a dog occasionally in hedges and similar inaccessible places, he didn't really like dogs. They killed rats, so that even if he was paid for catching them, he was only paid once. He preferred to catch them alive in his hands or in nets, or in stockings placed over the holes, because then he not only got paid for catching them, but could subsequently sell them to owners of rat pits or to people who wanted to train young dogs.

Once he had decided where the rats in our hedge were lying, he began to calculate which way they would go if they were disturbed and were to bolt. Certainly they would not risk a dash across the open if there was safety to be had by darting along the hedge-bottom or ditch, covered and protected by the density of the brambles and undergrowth; it was equally certain that they would do their best to improve their situation by moving to denser cover or some other more impregnable retreat. About thirty yards down the hill from the warren where these rats were lying was one of the 'pit holes' so beloved by farmers living in deep country, where refuse collection is no more than a distant urban convenience. Here was a hollow about thirty yards across, dug deep, in generations past, by farmers who needed the marl to spread upon their land. It remained a willow-fringed pit for years, holding a resident pair of water-hens on the water that drained there, the odd pair of mallard and a colony of rabbits in the banks. There were bicycle frames and bedsteads, rusty corrugated sheets and bottles, some hawthorn roots from a hedge long since grubbed out, and a mouldering feather-bed.

Any rats which succeeded in getting to this sanctuary would be safe even from the wiles of Hairy; however many ferrets he put down—and he rarely used more than four—there was enough cover for the rats to play hide-and-seek without ever taking the risk of emerging into the open.

The plan of campaign was to rattle about in the pit hole, to convince rats lying in holes further down the hedge that danger and not sanctuary lay that way; then to begin by putting the ferrets in holes nearest the pit hole so that rats could be driven away from it towards the bury down the hedge, where Hairy's naturalist-detective mind had deduced the main colony was hiding. As soon as a hole was clear and the ferrets emerged, he pressed the mouth in with his great hob-nailed boot, so that no rat, trying to get back later to the safety of the pit, could dive for cover on the way. At the same time he flattened the long grass and nettles in the hedge-bottom, so that there was no chance of escaping unseen.

There were also two gaps in the hedge, and Hairy produced bits of fine mesh string-netting from his pocket, cut sticks from the hedge about two feet long and as thick as his finger, and hung the netting at right-angles to the hedge and sticking two or three feet out each side, but suspended clear of the ground. Any rats that did try to escape along the cover of the hedge would pass safely under it on their way to the place we wanted them to hide, but would either be enmeshed or forced to run round into the open to avoid it when eventually it was pegged at ground-level and they were trying to return to safety.

The preliminaries of this, my first ratting expedition with my own dog, seemed very elaborate and rather boring; I wanted to see action. The previous night I had lain awake imagining Mick catching rats in a continuous cascade, like bottles from a juggler's hand. When sleep did eventually come, I dreamed he outshone all rat dogs there had ever been.

The substance was duller than the shadow. We had been half an hour banging about on the rubbish in the marl pit and then quickly ferreting up the hedgerow. The rats that had appeared merely slunk along the hedge-bottom towards the warren where Hairy had decided the main colony was lying. Our dogs were tied to stakes further down the hedge, because the idea was to scare the rats we moved as little as possible so that they would bolt again when the real fun started. If we had harried them too much at the outset they would have preferred to stay underground and fight it out with the ferrets rather than take the risk of meeting us again.

I often think that amateurs are distinguished from professionals less by differences of skill than by the trouble professionals take with details. When I do any carpentry, I am so impatient to get the job finished that nothing ever really fits; a professional may well take a greater number of hours on the same job, but he makes certain that each detail is accurate, and when he has finished, the whole thing bears the stamp of his craftsmanship.

Hairy was a craftsman with rats. Most amateurs, when they find 'worked' ratholes, throw the ferrets in, stand back and blame their luck when most of the rats escape. This didn't happen to Hairy: he would spend exactly as long as necessary, be it five minutes or fifteen, deciding which way his quarry would try to escape. He was a rat psychologist, with enough experience to think as rats would think. When he had decided which would be the most likely escape routes, he would calculate how they could best be blocked, so that the ones that he left would be the most exposed, and the only way to escape would be to run the gauntlet by coming into the open and giving his grasping hands a chance or, failing that, his sharp little terrier.

The very first day of my apprenticeship taught me that ratting, along with every other form of hunting, is a science. My impatience at seeing rats escape, even though temporarily, was almost intolerable, but my tutor displayed neither emotion nor excitement. He had a poker face, as impassive as parchment yellow with age. It was only when I knew him better that I learned to read the signs of excitement as his little eyes contracted smaller still.

At last he was satisfied that the hedge bank was clear from the pit to the main warren. He had filled in the holes, flattened as much of the rank undergrowth as he could without making a noise, and lowered the nets, so that nothing could get back without a diversion, one side or other, into open field. We fetched the dogs, and I was put on the far side of the hedge with old Mick, whilst Hairy and his terrier guarded the side he reckoned most rats would bolt.

The idea was that I should leave Mick loose to join in the fun when he felt like it, and that I should be personally responsible for driving any rats which bolted my side through to Hairy and his dog.

The old man put three ferrets in the main warren, crept a few yards along the hedge and crouched immobile as a scarecrow. Almost at once there was a thumping below ground and two beady eyes behind an enormous set of whiskers poked from a hole. The rat kept so still that the outline of his head was no more precise than the russet autumnal leaves scattered everywhere; only the glint of his eyes and the sensitive twitching of his nostrils gave him away. I lunged towards him with my stick, and he sank into the ground as silently as he had emerged, to be feet away before the blow struck.

Hairy had always been polite to me until then. I was 'the doctor's son' and was likely to give his expeditions an air of respectability: he hoped that I could give him the entrée to places where he was not welcome; he calculated that I could be quite an asset as a part-time, unpaid assistant ratcatcher. But he didn't suffer fools gladly. My clumsy blow at a rat not even clear of the safety of his hole had not had the slightest chance of success. All it had done was to warn it that danger outside was even greater than peril from the ferrets below ground, and he had returned to fight it out rather than take a further risk. The volley of oaths heaped on my head convinced me of my folly. It was years before I understood the exact meaning of some of the words, but the general gist was crystal clear. I was advised, in a tone I understood, even if I did not understand the subtlety of phrase, that young gentlemen should wait until it was too late for the rat to return to safety before making the slightest movement. He never used a stick himself. He liked to crouch close to the runs and grab a rat in his hands as it passed—or tried to pass.

I am quite certain that no Test cricketer, fielding in the slips, ever had such accurate, biddable hands. It was quite impossible to follow their exact movement with the eye, so that I never quite discovered precisely where he picked them up to avoid being bitten, but they very rarely managed to pinch him.

Within seconds of my ineffective onslaught a rat literally exploded from a hole his side of the hedge. It streaked for safety one moment and, in a split second, it had disappeared, but not to safety. No conjurer was quicker; one swift grab, and the rat was transferred to the murky depths inside his shirt. He popped two more into the same fastness before I discovered where they were going. Hairy's movements were as quick as sleight of hand, and when I did spot where he was putting them, I simply did not believe my eyes. The inside of one's shirt, after all, is a pretty unlikely spot to hide a live rat. Apart from the risk of being bitten, first thoughts would indicate that no rat would be likely to stay there long.

Hairy knew what he was at. His trousers were supported by a gigantic leather belt, so they could get no lower than that; his neck was tied round with a kerchief, and between the two the warmth and darkness gave the illusion of safety. So many a rat spent the first moments after capture snuggled with a ruck of its fellows against the maestro's belly. Indeed, he not only put them there until there was a lull in the sport and he could transfer them to the comparative security of a sack; he used to keep an odd one there for 'party tricks', to earn him a pint at the local.

So far I had got nothing but a string of oaths flung at my head; but soon the pace hotted up. As the ferrets found the main colony, rats shot out in every direction. Hairy got his shirt full, and his little dog caught most of those that he missed. My dog Mick had spent the first part of his life learning that he was not allowed to kill things. Ferrets were strictly forbidden, and so were fowls and ducks and sheep and cats. It naturally took some time to dawn on him that here, at last, was something that he was not only allowed, but positively encouraged to attack. For that reason, it is not a good thing to catch a grown rat and give it to a young dog in cold blood. He has probably been cuffed every time he has chased anything in the past, and if he does tentatively pick it up, and get bitten for his trouble, he is likely to assume it to be just punishment for illegal sport, and leave rats alone in future. Ours was the better way. As every rat that Hairy's dog caught squealed, the music was as moving to Mick as the swirl of bagpipes to a Highland warrior. He got more and more excited, making tentative lunges at every rat that passed, but always being beaten to the punch by his rival, who seemed to be both sides of the hedge at once. I was banging about with my stick, and ferrets and dogs were in almost as much danger as the quarry, though my marksmanship was such that all escaped.

Then a rat came out that looked as big as a rabbit. He streaked down my side of the hedge, and Mick, excited beyond endurance, made a dive that, from its very determination, was bound to succeed. At the last split second he must have had his doubts about whether he really was allowed to bite any harder than play, because though he picked it up all right, he didn't kill it.

The result was inevitable. The rat writhed round and sank half an inch of yellow fangs into the terrier's cheek. At that point, Hairy's advice paid off. Without the excitement, such a sensitive pup would have flinched and might never have touched another rat. But in hot blood the pain inflamed his passion more. Although he couldn't for the moment shake himself free and was wont to scream in agony at the sound of a harmless newspaper rattled near him, he made not the slightest sound. Instead, his jaws gripped tighter than a vice, crunching the breath from his quarry, until at last it was compelled to loose its hold. Then he started to shake, and he went on shaking in thudding, rhythmic revenge long after the dead rat had become as limp and shapeless as an old rag doll.

Mick had suddenly become a darting fury, with the fox terrier agility of his gentle mother and the toughness of the fighting bull terriers on his father's side. Rats continued to flee from the ferrets, and he did not get bitten again, though

15

he accounted for six or seven more. Nor did he waste time shaking more than was necessary again. One bite and a flick was all it took. No rat died quicker or more surely. His stumpy tail was up, and from then on there was nothing he would rather do.

Even Hairy was satisfied. It went against the grain to see good saleable rats killed, but he was genuinely delighted that the sacrifice had turned what he regarded as rather a 'nesh', or sensitively effete, little dog into a good working terrier. And anyway, there had been far more rats than he had expected, and he was able to transfer fourteen from his shirt to the comparative safety of a carrying-bag, and later to the ultimate security of his wire-net cage at home.

It was only the first lesson. Now that Mick had learned that he was positively encouraged to catch rats, he had to acquire the art of restraint. A dog which is too rumbustious and rushes all over the place is an unmitigated nuisance. It is just as bad for him not to let his quarry get clear of the hole, too far away to duck back to safety, as it was for me to aim my blow at a head which could disappear more quickly than I could ever strike.

We were both taught at the same time. The next excursion was not to 'break a dog in' but a strictly professional visit on which Hairy expected to earn hard cash.

A small poultry farmer was losing eggs and food to a colony of rats which had taken up quarters under the fowl-pens, and before we started a price was agreed of sixpence a grown rat and threepence a young one. The colour of the coat was to be the dividing line, for rats are grey-coated for the first weeks, and moult out brown when about a third of their full size. This was not a usual arrangement with Hairy, who not unnaturally preferred a 'tanner' a rat, irrespective of size. But the client had been caught once before, when a nest of sixteen had cost him eight shillings, although they were no bigger than mice. He had been assured that 'nits grow into lice', but remained adamant that either better terms were

16

agreed or he would have to poison them himself, which no good livestock-breeder likes to do.

I was introduced as 'this kid's the doctor's son—and he's got a good dog', and told to stop at one corner of a hen pen where I could watch an end and one side while he took care of the area in which they were most likely to bolt. I was told to 'hold the dog and don't loose him until the rats are well into the open', and if a ferret came out, I was to pick it up and put it in another hole.

He certainly knew what he was at. I didn't see a single rat whilst he caught twelve old ones, and a nest of six youngsters. Apprentices can't expect the most excitement, and I amused myself by making Mick sit without being held, and back away when a ferret showed up.

After that, I spent every spare minute of the holidays out ratting, and was very worried, when the time came to go back to school, to find that I must get rid of my ferret because nobody was prepared to look after it while I was away.

Hairy came to the rescue. He said that if I let him have it back, he would look after it, give it some work to keep it in practice, and I could collect it again on the first day of the next holidays.

No term ever dragged on longer. The very first day of the Christmas holidays I was round at the farm where Hairy kept his ferrets. The farmer gave him some milk for them on condition the place was kept free of rats for nothing. The hutch was at the back of a dark little dirt-floored fowlpen and, at that time of the year, was a uniform, sticky, green, oozing mire, where the hens paddled in and out to the rickyard, where they wisely spent the whole of their waking hours. I was greeted with the depressing news that my ferret had died from a rat bite but, although he was really very short at the moment, there was one wonderful quiet jill which he wouldn't sell to anybody else for gold. I could have her for three and sixpence.

My view was that, since my ferret had been killed catching

his rats, she should be replaced for nothing. While we were arguing I noticed old Mick—he was less than twelve months old in years, but already 'old in the head'—I noticed him working at a drain in the yard. He was crouched there, head on one side, silent and quivering with excitement.

'There's a rat in that drain,' I said.

'Hold your dog then.'

All bargaining ceased, a ferret was picked out of the dozen milling round in the hutch and popped down the far end of the pipe. Hairy replaced the dog and crouched over the other end.

A second later he had got him. Far from waiting for him to break clear of the hole, he scooped him up almost as soon as his shoulders were clear, and the ferret was retrieved with the other hand a second later.

'Now you'll see if they'm good ferrets,' he said.

He inched the door of the hutch open and popped the ferret in. Then he suddenly opened the other door, dropped the rat in and slammed it shut. There was one mad scramble, like a pack of forwards falling on top of a rugby scrum-half. A moment later, when they were beginning to eat it, Hairy said he must take it out. I never mind feeding my ferrets on healthy rats, especially if they are corn fed, but I suppose he had caught such a lot on refuse tips and other filthy places that he wouldn't let his ferrets eat a rat once they had cast their baby coat. In any case, rats are such carriers of jaundice that he was probably wise.

He opened the door and picked up the dead rat, to which four or five ferrets were hanging, shaking like bull terriers. The rest were milling round, looking for a space to grab. The inevitable happened, and one grabbed him right through the joint of his thumb.

Nobody who lacks first-hand experience can appreciate just how painful a ferret bite is. Four canine teeth, each as sharp as a needle, are driven home by muscle of incredible strength. It is said that the teeth of a ferret sink in until they meet. That

is an understatement. They sink in until they meet—and pass
—and interlock.

Hairy was slightly luckier. The ferret on his thumb could
not interlock its teeth because the bone of his knuckle prevented the teeth penetrating deeper. It must have been a bit
sharp for all that, but he didn't bat an eye. He let the other
ferrets pull their rat back into the hutch, calmly shut the door
and held his hand up for me to see. The ferret was still hanging
grimly on.

'It ain't savage,' he said. 'Got me by mistake. It was only
making a "put" at the rat.' He waited for my agreement
before putting a thumb on its skull, a horny finger under the
base of its tongue and calmly choking it off. It is not everyone
who is stoical enough to endure the agony of a ferret shaking
his flesh for longer than is absolutely necessary, rather than be
put at a disadvantage in subsequent bargaining. But he would
not risk having to argue with a prospective customer who
could claim some deduction because the ferrets were not
quiet.

Now that he had turned the tables he was justifiably pleased
with himself. He stroked the ferret lovingly, the pain of his
recent experience already forgotten. Judging by the poor
beast's protruding eyes, it could not efface so easily the
memory of its hairbreadth escape from strangulation. Then
he noticed that I was not giving my whole attention to the
deal. My eyes were fixed with horror on his mangled thumb,
which was dripping blood in a continuous stream. It probably
washed some of the poison from the wound, but it was a little
distracting.

With a grunt of impatience he bent, scooped a handful of
sticky green slime from the fowlpen floor, and slapped it, like
a plaster, on the offending member.

'There, kid,' he said, 'that'll stop it "blading".'

I was conquered. He got his three and sixpence for a ferret
to replace the one he had lost of mine. We did a great deal of
ratting that holiday and I picked up some of the tricks of the

trade. If he caught a nursing doe, he counted the teats the young were suckling and assessed that there was a nest containing that number of young. Then, when the time came to settle up, he would claim sixpence a rat for those he could show and threepence for each used teat of the does, on the grounds that 'the ferrets have killed and eaten the young', or that 'there is a nest of babies which are too young to fend for themselves and will starve'. The more knowledgeable of his clients wouldn't wear it, of course, and refused to pay for what they couldn't see. And even then it would often have paid them to check that the bags he brought were empty. The mugs paid up all they were asked without a murmur. Or most of them did. A story, which still lives about him in the district, tells of a notoriously mean solicitor who refused to pay his due and had a bagful of live rats emptied in his study, with the advice to catch them himself, then.

My attraction for him was that I often got him a bit of rabbiting which would otherwise have been forbidden. If we were on a farm he would say, when we had finished catching the rats, 'Gaffer, do you mind if we catch a rabbit or two while we're here? I'm trying to help the little lad by showing him how to go on a bit.'

'The little lad', by this time, was getting a pretty shrewd idea how to go on for himself, and, worse still, so was my terrier Mick. Indeed Mick, who had been the introduction at the outset, proved to be the stumbling-block on which our friendship eventually shattered. The trouble was that Mick got too good. He was as quick as an adder when he struck, showed even less emotion than the maestro on the now rare occasions when he got bitten and could kill about three rats while old Hairy was stuffing one in his shirt. His own dog only caught those which would otherwise have escaped, because it had learned from bitter experience that the area within reach of fist or boot was very unhealthy.

Mick would squeal at the sound of a folded newspaper, as much because it hurt his dignity as anything else. But when

Hairy cuffed him hard for catching a rat he reckoned was 'his', the young dog didn't understand. One moment he was encouraged by me, his master, to kill the brutes: the next he was clouted for trying to do just that. Besides which, his passion and tail were up, and the instinctive reaction to pain, in his hot blood, was to swap blow for blow. So he bit the old man's offending hand before he could withdraw it, and since there was no bargain at stake, he made more fuss about it than most ordinary folk would make if a ferret bit them.

The upshot was that I was told that, if I wanted to go ratting with him, I must leave my bloody dog at home.

The family was delighted. We were rather a respectable household, and it was considered not quite the thing for me to be seen trailing about with the local ratcatcher with a mongrel on a string in one hand and a bag of ferrets in the other. The climax had nearly been reached when Hairy had poked his head uninvited through the drawing-room window in the middle of a bevy of rather important guests and asked if 'young Philip was about'. So Mick got full marks for being the cause of a rift which never properly healed. When the guests were gone, I was told, in terms I could well understand, that in future Kelly must confine himself to the back door, ask for me and wait there until I arrived.

The family did not know Hairy. He may not have been rich, but he was certainly independent. If the front door was good enough for honoured guests, it was good enough for him. So he still called for 'young Philip', and each time he came he brought nearer the inevitable day when I should be flatly forbidden to meet him at all.

Had the family known of his 'party tricks' our friendship would never have blossomed so far. He was always willing, for the price of a pint or so at the local, to pop a ferret down the neck of his shirt to meet the inevitable rat he carried there, on the chance of finding a customer—he was so professional they should have been 'clients'—who wanted one alive to train a pup. His shirt would bubble and quake as they did noisy battle around his belly, until eventually there was the silence of death, broken only by the rather sickening crunch of cracking bones as the ferret started its supper. The ferret, of course, was always victorious, although it sometimes had a gaping gash to show for the price of its triumph.

For a slightly higher wager, he would tether a rat to the little round top of a pub table so that it was constricted to a circle of about a foot diameter, and take bets that he would kill it 'without the use of his hands'. When the stakes were high enough he would catch it like a terrier with his teeth, apparently utterly immune if a slight error of judgement, when he struck, resulted in a gash on his nose or cheeks.

But what fascinated me were his tricks of the trade. The eye of his experience would assess *exactly* where the rats were most likely to bolt, and he would crouch there, shapeless as a wet old sack, with no tremor of movement to betray him, and 'field' rat after rat as it made a vain bid for freedom. He knew exactly where to post any dogs that were allowed out, so that they were far enough from the hole to avoid frightening their quarry back underground but near enough to intercept with certainty.

His ferrets were always perfect too. Slim and hard and agile. Never fat, but never hungry enough to stay below and feed if they killed or found a nest of young. They hunted for the love of killing, and would kill and kill and kill again, despite the fact that he broke all the rules of ferret keeping. They should have a warm, dry nest box to sleep in, but their run should be as large and airy as possible so that there is scope for ample exercise. His ferrets lived in a fetid little hutch, and they got a lot of bread and milk, because he happened to have access to free milk from the farm where he kept them. The fact that they got all the exercise they wanted, and more than they needed, compensated for the lack of space in their quarters, and the young and nestling rats they caught were a perfect natural diet.

He was an artist, too, at knowing his own—and his ferrets'

—limitations. Rats come in from the fields in September and October, when food gets scarce and the weather threatens wet and cold. In my day there were no combine harvesters, and corn was kept in the rick and sometimes not threshed out until late in the spring.

So every rick had its colony of rats. At first they would get among the baulks of timber and straw which formed the foundation, and then they would make tunnels, a foot or so in from the sides, up to the top, where they would often take up residence just under the thatch. In the evening I have often stood quite quietly in a rickyard, listening to them setting up home almost within reach of the surface. If I plunged a muck fork or iron bar towards the seat of the noise the rat would often jump for safety into the open, making a target for old Mick in the process.

Up to that stage Hairy was always willing to ferret a rick, and he would put half a dozen ferrets in at various points and usually catch most of the rats that were there.

Sooner or later, depending on the number of rats in the colony and the time they had been there, they would tunnel deeper and deeper into the rick until it was riddled as full of holes as a honeycomb. It was useless ferreting then. The rats would just play hide-and-seek and never come out, but occasionally one would be caught in a tunnel between two ferrets and pay the penalty unheralded and unmourned. No movement on the surface often indicated that one of the ferrets had stayed to dine on the dead rat, while we sportsmen outside waited, with what patience we could muster, until the ferret saw fit to emerge.

Hairy knew too much about the game to be easily persuaded to ferret a rick once the rats were working deep towards its heart. But the fact that he knew he was beaten did not constrain him to admit it, and his plausible tongue would skate over so many reasons, good from the client's viewpoint, why he should keep his ferrets in their bag.

Once he had given me the groundwork, I didn't mind

going out to catch my rats alone. At least, that way, there was no one to complain about old Mick killing too many, and I have always been fascinated by watching any dog work, be it a terrier or gundog, sheepdog or guard.

Luckily he took to the game far more quickly than I did and certainly taught me more than I taught him. His chief virtue, in addition to his toughness and enthusiasm, was that he was naturally cunning and steady. It is very difficult to make most dogs sit quietly a good six feet from a rathole, when they can hear the ferrets bustling them about below ground. They dash to the nearest hole, thrust their snout down it and, with one puff of breath, persuade their quarry to stay below and fight it out with the ferrets they know, rather than risk an encounter with the dog they do not. Mick learnt very soon that if he crouched clear of the hole, as the maestro, Hairy, always did, it was much easier to catch his rats in the open.

He went one stage better. It is normally impossible to ferret under a building such as a fowlpen without an assistant. By standing at diagonally opposite corners it is possible for each to see an end and a side, so that apart from losing rats one doesn't see bolt, there is no possibility of the ferret coming out unnoticed and sneaking off to do damage in the poultry yard. I could manage with Mick. I would sit him at a corner, where he could see two sides, and go to the opposite corner myself.

He would catch anything which bolted his side, and if a ferret came out, he would come straight round to me with a sheepish, hangdog sort of expression, as if it were his fault. I knew that he never came unless he considered something had gone wrong, and I could be quite sure that no ferret would wander off out of my sight without Mick giving me due warning.

For my part I was soon pretty proficient, though I did not get such a high percentage of kills as he did. I had learnt from Hairy to assess the padded runs accurately enough to place the nets fairly astutely, and I became an inveterate scrounger of ladies' discarded stockings. There were no sheer nylons about then. Ladies' stockings were still strong, and fairly thick. I used to twist a piece of stout, galvanized fencing-wire into a loop to fit the top end, like the mouth of a butterfly net, and peg this over a likely rathole. I cut the foot of the stocking up and tied the end with string.

It was rather like coarse fishing. The first sign is an almost imperceptible bulge at the mouth of the stocking. The rat is probing to find if this strange, dark tunnel, with soft sides, is a way of escape. He generally sits for a few seconds at the mouth of the hole, gently nudging the stocking while he makes up his mind. It corresponds to the period in fishing when the fish is just 'nibbling' the bait. Strike then, and he will swim away frightened but unscathed. A moment's patience, and he will swallow the hook. The rat's next move, provided that men and dogs have made no sign that they know he is there, will be a dramatic dash. Suddenly a lump will project itself down the leg of the stocking, to be brought up short where it is tied at the ankle. It will writhe and bubble in panic, and then usually subside into silence and stillness. When the rat discovers his escape is barred he erupts into frenzy, and then, far quicker than it would take to dawn on most men, he realizes that the worst has not happened; that his enemies apparently have not discovered his discomfiture and that the clever thing to do is to freeze into immobility while assessing the lie of the land. That is the moment to put your foot on the stocking to prevent the rat returning or the ferret following him up, for she will be cut unnecessarily if she does. Then, at leisure, tie a piece of string behind him to keep him in, or undo the string at the end and decant him into a wire rat cage or a bag. If he is not wanted alive a good clout with a stick will settle his final account.

I grew quite clever with stockings and a fair shot with a stick. I was never the least use at hockey or any ball game at school, and it was thought that the reason was that the Lord had not endowed me with a 'straight eye'. But I could stop a rat in full stride with a thatching peg—or indeed any stick that was properly balanced—almost as certainly as Hairy could scoop one up with his greedy hands. It was not that I had a natural eye for rats and not for hockey balls, but simply that my heart was never in organized games.

Hairy was not only good at putting a stocking over exactly the right ratholes, but he could set a net with supreme artistry too. He usually put it at right-angles to the run, but the trick lay in gauging the exact degree of tautness. Too taut, and it might as well have been wire netting, so open was the invitation to circumvent it; and too loose was worse still. The first rat in got in such a tangle that the rest escaped while he was being disentangled. I never became proficient with rat nets, although I could set a purse net for rabbits with the next. Indeed, rat nets were another bone of contention between the old man and me. He complained enough when Mick killed a rat he thought he could have caught alive, but when he bundled into a net and knocked it down so that the quarry escaped, or, worse still, killed one while it was enmeshed, tearing the net in the process, the language that spilled about our ears was almost tangible.

My ineptitude with nets was a major cause of my subsequent passion for seeing dogs work. I took no particular pride in my part of the proceedings, so that I could give myself up to the admiration of a clever dog—particularly if I had trained him.

Any dog which does much ratting gets bitten occasionally, and my experience is that folk who boast that their dog never gets bitten either do very little ratting or have a shy dog which will not take any risks. A clever dog never gets bitten unnecessarily. If the rat is in the open and there is time, he collars him across the shoulders and either crushes or shakes, and all is quickly over. But a rat often crouches between sacks of corn or in some more or less inaccessible corner, and faces all comers. Or it so nearly escapes that only an inch of backside is there to be bitten—and when pulled clear, the business end is free to retaliate. A game dog makes the most of his chances and almost certainly gets bitten in the process.

I did not appreciate how dauntless a game dog was until I had been well and truly bitten myself. There was a low bank running alongside a rickyard full of corn, and the rats had riddled it with holes and were lying deep in the dry earth until they had had time to make their workings in the rick.

It was, in theory, an ideally easy place to ferret. Every rat that bolted would try to get into a hole in the rick, a short ten feet across the cart track. So I moved quietly along the rick, stuffing a handful of straw into every hole. Now, when a rat bolted across the track, it would be baulked by the blocks I had put in the holes and fall easy prey to Mick or to me and my stick.

I started at one end of the bank, meaning to fill in the holes and make the bank good as the ferret worked, so that, as we moved along, we left behind us only blocked holes which offered no sanctuary. But when I put my ferret in the first hole, she disappeared—and that was that. The bank was low enough for me to see both sides, and I was standing at one end, so that I was perfectly certain that she had not come out and wandered off. Unless the gap is very small, there is not much fear of the ferret going off unnoticed, because in spite of an ability to move like an adder's strike, when in combat with a rat, ferrets have a peculiarly aimless, shortsighted gait when exploring territory in which they are not particularly interested.

I waited ten minutes in the certainty that my ferret had not wandered off, during which time there was neither sight nor sound of a rat. I had made Mick sit at the far end of the bank, fifty yards or so away, to take care of anything trying to escape that way, and he was still crouching there, shivering as he always did with excitement, ears cocked and his stump of a tail gently waving, almost as if in response to the slight breeze. Ten minutes more and I had stretched full-length with my ear to the hole the ferret had entered, but there was no sound at all.

You cannot enjoy any kind of sport associated with working dogs unless you are possessed of a fair amount of patience. Certainly it is one of the very few virtues with which I happen to have been endowed, and time never troubles me much, nor do I let the clock 'gaffer' me. But within half an hour I was not so much impatient as worried about the fate of my ferret. A constant danger, when one is ferreting round farm buildings, is that the holes rats have excavated and are using are connected to the old drainage system. If they are, it is quite possible for the ferret to get into some old land drain, without ever showing on the surface after she has entered the bury, and for her to wander below ground for a couple of hundred yards before emerging, still unseen and unseeable, in the thicket surrounding some fetid farm pool or overgrown ditch. If she does, she can get into all sorts of mischief or danger.

My imagination began to suggest all sorts of fates for my ferret. She was probably not in the bank I was watching so patiently at all, but already creating carnage in the poultry pens. Or she would come up in the stockyard, panic the bullocks and get trampled to death. Least likely, but most frightening of all, she was perhaps stuck in some narrow hole and would die of starvation.

The idea appalled me. I thrust my hand up the hole where she had disappeared to probe and try to find her. Naturally I could reach only about nine inches, even with my small, boyish hand, and could feel nothing. I tried every hole along the bank as far as old Mick, but still drew blank. Leaving Mick to hold the fort, I prowled round the rickyard in the forlorn hope that she had emerged, unseen, and was wandering about. Nothing kills patience like worry, and I came back to have one more try at the holes. In retrospect, I can think of nothing more foolish than sticking questing fingers into ratholes when a ferret is there and there is the least chance of

28

a rat sharing the same quarters. However quiet she is—and since the first keeper's ferret bit me I have taken care to have amenable ferrets—it is never sensible to handle her without due care immediately after she has been thoroughly roused in battle with a rat.

Closer search revealed a hole, apparently unused and unworn, right at the end of the bank. It was, in fact, a 'bolt hole', opened accidentally from the interior of the bury, as the rats enlarged it from the inside. Rabbits make bolt holes in the same manner, and rarely use them except for escape in an emergency. They are unobtrusive, the very holes likely to be missed when nets are put down, and by the time they become obvious it is usually too late, as the rat or rabbit has escaped. My inexperience had failed to discover this bolt hole each time I had looked before, and when I did find it, I shoved my questing fingers boldly into the depths of the bank.

It was a painful mistake. I was galvanized by a sharp, searing stab each side of my thumb, and the pain became more excruciating as the grip tightened. The silence of the rickyard echoed to my uninhibited screams, as I struggled to withdraw my hand. But the harder I pulled, the more intense the agony—and I was unable to budge as much as half an inch. A farm labourer ambled round the corner of the rick, as if tomorrow would do, to see what all the fuss was about; and he was obviously mystified. There was a small boy, one hand rigidly on—or just in—the ground, using it as a pivot as he convulsed himself round it screaming until his lungs would burst. It must have looked like some weird dance, some ritual feat, the object of which was to form the most extraordinary contortions around one arm which must remain rigid and motionless. The labourer surveyed the scene in wonderment for some seconds, before he discovered that the noise was not the ecstatic scream of some new pop song but a symptom of genuine anguish.

'What's up, kid?' he said.

'The ferret's got my thumb,' I howled. 'Get him off.'

And then he moved quite fast. He sized up the geography of the problem, dived into an adjacent shed and reappeared with a fork. Strong sweeps crumbled away the turf and earth of the bank, exposing the hole and my hand. There, with yellow fangs buried to the roots, beady black eyes evil and defiant, was the largest rat I had ever seen. To me he looked, and felt, bigger and stronger than a lion. Although the hole was opened quite wide enough for him to escape, he made no apparent attempt to do so, but hung on to my thumb like a bulldog. The labourer wasted no time, but drove a prong of his fork clean through the rat's chest, impaling him to the ground. In his dying convulsion he loosed my thumb to gnaw at the hard steel.

The relief was unbelievable. I suppose he had held me fast for the best part of a minute, but even at this distance of time, the pain is so vivid that it might have been for hours. As I tried to suck out the poison with the pulsing blood, I watched the labourer scoop away more bank, and there was my ferret hanging doggedly on to the rat's haunch. That explained why he had not bolted. He had paused at the bolt hole and noticed me within striking distance, so had bided his time for a moment of safety to make a dash.

His indecision had cost him his life and me, it felt, my thumb. The ferret had followed and managed to get a good mouthful of the equivalent of rat ham. The hole was too narrow for the rat to turn round to fight it out, and when the ferret had splayed her legs they had both stuck solidly in the hole, the rat's head being within six inches of fresh air and freedom. And there they had both jammed, until my foolish thumb had been shoved literally into the jaws of the rat to complete the stalemate.

It certainly taught me a lesson about putting my hand in holes where rats were lying—and it finished my ratting for the day. It also taught me how much more painful a rat bite is than a ferret's, because it hurts so much more afterwards.

The top fangs had gone clean through my thumb nail and met the bottom teeth on the bone, and as time went on the pain became more, rather than less, acute, because there was no room for my flesh to swell under the nail. I had poultices on all night, and I vowed to myself that there must be some more amusing and less painful way of spending the holidays.

Subsequent loves draw a veil of nostalgia over previous travail, and when my pain had gone I was ready to try again. The chap who had rescued me had been full of praise for the steadiness of my dog and the steadfastness of my ferret, and nothing seduces the sportsman more irresistibly than praise of the dog he has trained. Mick had become extremely quick, and the bull terrier in him made him as careless of pain as I was of time. It did not matter to him whether a rat was coming or going, whether he could only see a tiny scrap of fur in the crevice or mouth of a hole—he grabbed it. If it was able to bite him in reply he simply crushed it harder and more surely. He would rather have a day ratting than anything else in the world—and I was in complete sympathy. His nose was sensitive and accurate as a bloodhound's. He would be loafing along a hedgerow, to all appearances wool-gathering, when he would suddenly freeze into immobility. One forefoot would lift, his head tilt and his tail begin to quiver. As delicately as a cat, he would creep forward, his nostrils testing the eddies of air rising from the hole he suspected. He did not get excited and betray the degree of danger by puffing down occupied holes; rather the reverse, for he would just back away, sit down as delicately as an old maid on a damp chair, and implore me to pop the ferret in—quickly! As a result, we became very proficient and somewhat of a novelty. Farmers and poultrymen found it amusing to tell each other that they did not need to employ a professional ratcatcher because 'a kid of about twelve came round with a mongrel and cleared the lot out'. It suited me fine, because I had invitations to go to most of the farms in the district whenever I liked. I was invited indoors for dinner, and stuffed myself with vast quantities of rich farm food; and Mick had the honoured place by the kitchen fire, while the farm dogs were banished outside. I made friends who have stood me in good stead for the rest of my life, and I got a grounding in country lore which has been invaluable to me as a naturalist.

2. Mixed Company

By no means all the fun I had with Mick had to do with rats. He was the introduction to all sorts of people, like the old man who lived quite near, and earned his living hawking herbs all over the Black Country, where he was universally known as 'Austin th' 'erb Mon'. He was tall and loose-limbed and two things about him stand out vividly in my memory. One was that he had two quite separate rows of teeth, both top and bottom, which, in theory, should have endowed him with an aspect as ferocious as a pike or a crocodile. In fact, his blue eyes were always puckered with mischief and an almost continuous chuckle bubbled from his throat. The other striking feature, when you knew him, was the length of his beard. It never protruded from his leathery, weather-beaten face more than a quarter of an inch—and never less. He obviously never shaved, and yet the beard never seemed to grow long enough to be trimmed.

There were other things about 'Owd Austin to fire a boy's imagination, although they were not immediately so obvious. His right wrist, for instance, still bore the swollen callous where he broke it in a fight with a gypsy. And he was so ruggedly powerful that it seemed quite impossible that any gypsy could have withstood such a blow and survived. But

33

fear of offending him always prevented me from asking. He rode an immense bone-shaking old bicycle with a sack balanced through the frame which held coal dredged from the canal, or herbs to be hawked, or potatoes to be sold in the little shop at the back of his house, or even rabbits and birds he had shot. He owned a steam traction-engine which used to drag a threshing tackle from farm to farm in winter when his herbs were out of season, and it was through his profession as threshing-machine owner and operator that I came to know him.

I loved to turn up at a farm when they were threshing a rick which had become infested with rats, because when they got to the bottom, the sport was so fast and furious that it tested the skill and courage of the gamest dog and the aim of the best chap with a stick. I have helped catch several hundred in an hour or so; I once saw a huge rat take refuge up the trouser leg of an extremely excitable man—or he appeared to me unduly excitable, as the rat was only seeking sanctuary and was not bent on emasculation. I found ratting a very exciting occupation.

'Owd Austin and Mick formed a spontaneous friendship in which I shared. Over a bottle of cold tea and some bread and cheese he told me of his vendetta with the gypsies and stories of poaching that fired my imagination; so that when he invited me to go to his field the next Sunday morning and to see his gun, I was delighted.

His field commanded a unique position. It was isolated in the midst of surrounding farmland, and on this ten acres he grew enough sage and thyme and mint and parsley to hawk all over the Black Country.

When I got there the first thing he asked me was whether my terrier was broken to the gun. I told him that he had never heard one go off, so he asked me to get through the hedge, go round to the end of his field, and walk a long strip of sage back to him, letting the old dog work, in case there was a rabbit in it.

There was not, but a covey of partridge got up, going nicely to him—and one paid the penalty. A moment later a hare went out and he took not the slightest notice, so I assumed he had not seen it; but he shouted to me to stand still until he had loaded the gun.

I had never seen a muzzle loader before, nor have I met anyone since who owned one for anything other than ornament.

Austin popped in wads and powder and shot, ramming the whole lot with his steel ramrod as he went along, and the speed and dexterity he displayed had to be seen to be believed. When he let the thing off there was a bright orange flash and puff of smoke that would put most fireworks to shame. And when the haze cleared, it was surprising how often his quarry lay crumpled up.

After that I often took Mick on a Sunday morning, and as we got to know each other my duties extended. At first I would walk each patch of herbs in turn for him, but later I was sent for a walk in the surrounding farmland. I was young enough, and looked innocent enough, to rouse no suspicion, and I learnt a great deal about how to drive birds, game birds and hares and rabbits in the direction I wanted them to go. Perhaps that is an exaggeration. Austin knew, from previous experience, from the pattern and state of crops outside his field and from the state of the weather, which way they would *like* to go. He would then position himself on their flightline, and I would get behind them and walk them up to put the right idea in their heads, and to flush them in the desired direction. Before that, the drill was that I should take Mick for a walk, a nice innocent walk, round the adjoining farms, trying to flush every bird I could into Austin's cover. He would sit quietly marking, so that he knew how many there were and, if possible, just where they were. The final operation was for me to flush them in as small numbers as possible to allow him to reload between shots.

35

My reward was the loan of his gun. I had never let off anything more lethal than an air-rifle before. Austin had had a gun in his hand for so many years that he had almost forgotten that holding a gun tight was not a normal reflex action.

I watched, fascinated, as he poured his black powder in down the barrel, contained it with a wad and rammed it solid. My fears that the blows of the ramrod would ignite the charge and that it would sail off like a lethal great arrow into space were ungrounded. He put in the shot, another wad, rammed that, placed the percussion-cap, and all was ready for my first big bang.

About the only moving thing left, after I had driven every patch of cover in the district and he had shot everything worth shooting, was a flock of fieldfares. So far as I remember they were not protected in those days, and in Austin's field, lost at the Back of Beyond, I doubt if it would have made the slightest difference if they were. My object at the moment was to get something, almost anything, in the sights and have a shot.

I crouched and crept quietly from bush to bush along the hedge, never quite stopping but never moving suddenly. The secret in getting close to most wild things is soft stealth. They take almost as little notice of some apparently inanimate object which slides along as if it was still. But the first staccato movement will alarm them. Gradually I got within seventy yards and sixty and fifty of the rowan-tree where they were feeding. I raised the great gun, which was about as much as I could lift, at arm's length, and squinted along the sights. There was no question of the sportsmanship of shooting only at birds on the wing. They sat still in a cluster, but I was not strong enough to hold the gun steady, and the muzzle waved rhythmically, as if cushioned on the wave of my frailty, so that my target came into line with the sights only for a split second each time my gun oscillated past it.

Those birds were pretty safe. I was determined to get

36

something in the bag if I could, but the more I delayed pulling the trigger, the wider my relaxing muscles made me swing. When I did let it off there was a blinding flash, a puff of black smoke, a shooting agony in my shoulder—and I was flat on my back. My first reaction was that the gun had exploded and that my shoulder had taken the charge instead of the birds. I touched it gingerly for signs of blood or a shattered bone, but it was only terribly bruised. The gun was perfectly sound, but I had ignored Austin's advice. He had told me, whatever I did, to hold it tight, assuming I knew he had meant hold the butt tight into my shoulder. I thought he meant grip the barrel tight in my hand. He had been very liberal with the powder, determined I should kill at my first shot, so that the old weapon packed a kick that would not disgrace a hefty mule. In my excitement I had let the butt wander a good inch clear of my shoulder, so that when the charge did explode, the gun kicked back at me with almost as much velocity as registered in the shot leaving the barrel; and certainly with more effect, for I was the only casualty. I picked myself up and decided that I preferred watching Mick work to any amount of sport with a gun.

That is the only time I have fired a muzzle loader, but it did nothing to damp my enthusiasm for spending what hours I could with 'Owd Austin. He had the highest regard for Mick's ability as a driver of game, and we spent long hours working the beds of sage and thyme for rabbits and partridge and the occasional hare. He told me tales of poaching with his twin brother that were far more gripping than the books of adventure in foreign lands which cluttered my room in unread piles each time I had a birthday. Better still, he taught me some of the country arts that are dying now, killed by professional football and television and all the spoonfed entertainments that are stifling men's will to entertain themselves. I learned that 'a hang' is much more deadly set for a rabbit in a run in the open than placed ever so carefully in the run where he pops through the hedge. Austin made his own hangs from many-stranded brass wire, into which he wove the eyelets from old boots, making the noose run sweeter. He taught me to use every scrap of hedge or rising ground so that I was never silhouetted against the skyline, because it is so much harder to spot anyone walking against a dark background.

He had spent a lifetime moving about the countryside as stealthily as his own huge shadow. I took it for granted at first, until he chided me for making so much noise. He was two or three times as heavy as I was, he wore great nail-studded boots and yet, creep on tiptoe as I might, I always made more noise. When I watched him I saw that it was not altogether how hard he trod that was his secret. He kept his knees slightly bent, using them as springs, instead of walking tiptoe, and he seemed to notice twigs by instinct, so that his footsteps hardly ever broke or crushed anything that crackled. Boys are wonderful mimics. Instead of wanting to play Red Indians or soldiers, I amused myself copying Austin. It is often said than an only child is at a great disadvantage, especially if there are not many other children locally with whom he can play. It was a deficiency which never occurred to me, and if I could have my childhood again, it is something I would not alter. Growing up with countrymen like Hairy and Austin, who never craved company other than their own, I learnt the art of patience, and that one of the most exciting of all pastimes in the country is to wander and sometimes to wait and simply watch what happens. I loved the company of my dog, and would go off all day into the woods and fields without the least wish to break the satisfying silence by conversation. Instead of being distracted by small talk, I had time to watch how Mick amused himself. I saw him moving casually, apparently aimlessly, in the luxury of letting his sensitive nose question every subtle, shifting breeze. When something exciting was anywhere within yards, his whole attitude changed. The satisfying thing to me was that I had plenty of prior warning of an opportunity to observe

38

something I should not otherwise have seen. Mick would know that a rabbit or rat or hare or stoat was somewhere about, but he still did not know quite where. His stump of a tail would wag, the rapidity of its movement increasing, like a geiger counter, as he approached his quarry. It was like 'Hunt the Thimble', for I could read the signs as he got 'warmer'. Nothing helped my powers of observation so much. By watching him, I could see in which direction I should concentrate. Dogs can see moving objects clearly but cannot focus something which remains motionless and blends, by protective coloration, with its background. My eyesight was far more acute, but as yet untrained. Walking alone I would see little more than Mick would, because I did not know where to look and because animals and birds which are coloured protectively are not easy to spot, even with sharp eyes. Mick's nose gave me the clues when to be on the alert and in which direction to concentrate my search. That helped me to spot the glint of a dark eye or the little differences in pattern where some bird or animal merged into its background.

Although I took every advantage I could by watching Mick's mounting enthusiasm, I never reciprocated by telling him when I discovered the object of his search. Instead I let him hunt on himself, noting the type of place where he went wrong, the exact degrees by which his ardour mounted as he got 'warmer', and how close his quarry would sit before finally making a dash for freedom. Only if he failed and gave up did I lay him on the right line again, or give him enough clues to carry on himself. I see so many professional huntsmen 'lift' their hounds at the slightest check—or with no check at all—in order to short-circuit the chase and take advantage of the fact that some member of the field has seen the fox or hare and told him where it has gone. To my mind this is the type of unsporting practice which lends weight to the arguments of cranks, who would abolish all field sports if they could; and it certainly is very bad for hounds. As soon as they lose their line, they will fall back on their huntsman to help them out, instead of puzzling it out for themselves, and when the huntsman is not lucky enough to be told by a follower where his quarry has gone, he will be a broken reed.

Mick never got such help, and he grew up self-reliant. When he lost his line he would cast in bigger and bigger circles to try to recover it. If he found a rabbit in a bush he remembered it, and would try there again, even if it had been two years since he passed that way; and he built up in the back of his mind a store of likely sorts of places, so that he knew where it was sensible to try and where he would probably be wasting his time.

I was never very worried whether he caught his rat or rabbit, so that I found as much enjoyment in his failures as his successes. My reward was an accumulation of experience of where to look and what the reactions would be of whatever quarry interested him. When I spotted a rabbit in a 'sit', I was careful to avert my eyes at once and look at it, henceforth, obliquely, as girls look at men when they are shy—or pretend to be. Once a rabbit or hare catches your eye and knows for certain you have seen it, it will usually get up and go, with good reason, as if all the fiends of hell are on its scut. But provided I had not been gauche enough to betray my interest, I could watch the whole drama unfold. I could watch the mounting tension as the terrier worked gradually closer, the moment of indecision when it still seemed possible that fate would pass harmlessly by—if uncomfortably close—and the moment of truth when a dash for safety became inevitable.

If the dash took the dog by surprise, the split second it needed to register generally damped all hope of capture, for Mick, even in his prime, was never as fast as a rabbit on a fair run. But sometimes he would 'mark' in a reed tussock or bramble. His quarry would sit tight and Mick would freeze, as picturesque, to my eyes, as the most highly bred pointer. His forefoot would be raised in question, his quivering tail stilled for a moment, while ears and nose strained to pin-point his quarry. He knew, to within a foot or so, where it was. Often he could both hear and smell it breathing, but was still too uncertain of the exact spot to risk springing, landing in the wrong place—and missing it. Then he would circle warily, listening and sniffing and watching for movement, often 'setting' it again two or three times, as he took precise geometric bearings.

It was a fascinating duel to watch. A cold psychological war of nerves, which either attacker or victim could lose by premature movement. Experience taught Mick to make a very high percentage of captures by accurate location and a determined spring, and I learnt, as I watched his knowledge swell, so that I could often pick a rabbit up in a 'sit' myself. My eyesight made up for some of my deficiencies of hearing and scent, and when I spotted one, I found it fairly simple to walk close to it, as if I had not noticed, and pick it up in one smooth sweep at the last moment. The least hesitation or change of step gave the show away, so that the rabbit was yards out of reach before I could complete my stoop. Even when I was successful, I didn't always manage to hang on, because a rabbit is a pretty tricky handful until he is disarmed by grabbing his powerful, ripping back feet.

Watching Mick fail, when I knew where his quarry was, helped enormously when both of us were baffled. I gradually learned the art of thinking like a hunted animal, of being able to put myself in its place, and decide what I would do to elude pursuers if I was being hunted: whether to sit tight or make a dash for it; which way would give me the best chance of escape, for sometimes the short-term advantage of nearby cover would be outweighed by taking a longer chance, in the hope of getting to an adequate bury or thick cover at some distance away. Then, when Mick was puzzled, I could make constructive suggestions about where to try, or place myself between the area he was hunting and the most attractive escape route. We developed a wonderful partnership, and could almost read each other's thoughts. Although he was naturally an easy dog to train, discipline became superfluous. He knew that we were both trying for the same objective, and he grew to trust my judgement almost as implicitly as I trusted his wonderful nose. As a result he would react to my slightest movement as readily as a field trial gundog obeys the signals of his handler.

He used to be bitten by rats fairly often, not because he was inept but because he would risk grabbing anywhere rather than lose one. Normally he was bitten on the nose or lips and no great damage was done, except to the rat in retribution; but he did once get a bite which might have been very serious. He pulled a rat out by its backside from under some loose straw, and it turned and slashed him right across the eye. Luckily it did not actually puncture the eyeball, but put a deep scratch right across the sight. I took him to the local vet, who took a great deal of trouble cleansing and dressing and making it more comfortable.

When he was done I inquired what I owed. The vet looked me up and down, finding no doubt a rather shy and very worried small boy.

'If I charged what he's worth to you,' he said, 'you couldn't afford to pay me. If I charged what he's worth to anyone else, it would be nothing at all. I'll settle for a shilling.'

I think that summed up Mick's value and the value of all dogs which are kept for their companionship and their use. It is an insult to assess their worth in terms of cash, because money will not buy such loyalty and friendship and joy as they give. Pedigree dogs may be worth many times as much in market value, but the most valuable dog in the world gave no more joy to his owner than my old Mick gave me.

He was the ideal kind of teacher. He taught me to teach myself about country things, and he was an introduction to country folk of every social level. About three miles from my home was a large estate which had belonged to the

Vernon family for centuries. When I first remember it there were about six thousand acres, although that meant nothing to me at the time, because I was only five years old. The Squire was a patient of my father, and one of the most vivid memories of my childhood was being taken there in the car while my father was on a professional visit. I was left outside the front door, sitting in the car, and looking over what was the largest expanse of closely mown lawn I had ever seen; and as I gazed out over it, I suddenly noticed that there were dozens of rabbits grazing and playing beneath the great trees on the edge of the lawn.

When my father came down the steps from the Hall, accompanied by the Squire, I could contain myself no longer.

'Dad,' I said, 'ask him if I can have one of those rabbits.' He was a bearded, dapper, rather forbidding figure.

'What did the lad say?' he inquired.

'He wants one of your rabbits,' my father replied.

'Right,' said the Squire, 'next time you come, bring some salt and put it on their tails. You can have all you catch.'

It is extraordinary how stupid grown-ups take children to be. They were the first rabbits that I ever remember seeing, and they made so much impression on me that I can see them now, forty-five years later, almost as clearly as I did on that first day.

About six years later, when Mick was getting useful, I remembered them again. The old Squire had died and been replaced by his son. The estate had been frittered away by death duties to about two thousand acres, but the lawns and park around the house were just the same. My father introduced me to the new Squire, who was interested in my absorption with ferrets but not so enthusiastic about the dog. Shooting men of his generation believed that, if a strange dog, particularly an 'uncontrollable' terrier, galloped across their park, that would be the end of their pheasants and partridges.

However, I turned up, in answer to his invitation to a day's rabbiting, complete with my ferret and my dog, which I was promptly told to keep on the lead. I tied him to my belt, feeling somewhat subdued by my first really personal contact with the aristocracy, and we set off into the park. It was rolling, acid, rushy turf, rank with generations of neglect. Great belts of woodland, serving as pheasant and fox coverts, strewn with rhododendrons and shrubs, flanked it. There were a number of small plantations, fifty to a hundred yards square, carefully sited to give a wonderful view from the house; and flushing-points for pheasants, cover for rabbits and shelter for the guns.

In those days rabbits were valued, even by landowners and farmers, for the sport they gave, the food they provided and the aesthetic pleasure they gave to all who loved the country-side. Hilton Park was a paradise for them. The grass was so rank and rushy that they did little damage, and even at pre-war prices, the income they brought in was probably more than the cattle that grazed it provided.

From my point of view it was ideal. The big woods held vast warrens quite impractical to ferret, but a constant reservoir from which surplus rabbits spilled out into a host of small warrens, mostly started at night as 'play holes'. The place was keepered and relatively undisturbed, so that there were usually a few rabbits spending the day in these small buries, right out in the open parkland.

I discovered the ideal technique by accident on my first visit. I was not yet strong enough to dig, and the Squire preferred exercise more suitable to his station, so I did not use my ferret loose. Instead I put a collar on her and ten yards of strong, flexible whipcord. Already I knew the value of silence and how to use the wind, and so did Mick. The Squire nodded to me to try a small bury with no more than five or six holes, with only a few holes covering an area five or six yards across. Mick and I crept quietly upwind to it and he started to shiver with excitement. I put the ferret in the nearest hole, paying out line as she explored further away from me. The Squire stood quietly twenty yards away. There was a rumbling, like some far-off train approaching the platform of a London tube station, and three rabbits exploded into the sunlight at the same instant. Two shots from the Squire had a right and a left, while poor Mick turned somersaults at the end of his lead in his frantic efforts to give chase to a third. His one fault was what gypsies call 'opening up' and betraying their presence. That is to say, when giving chase, or trying to, he gave tongue in a eunuch's falsetto— though he was no eunuch, by any standards, as the owner of any local bitch discovered to his cost. This high-pitched yapping while his quarry was in sight worried the Squire a good deal more than it bothered me, because he was in constant fear that his pheasants would be frightened and wander over his boundaries; so when I discovered that it might lose my sport, I was able to cure it easily by a few heavy-handed cuffs to distract his attention.

When no more rabbits appeared, I retrieved the ferret by the simple expedient of pulling her gently from the hole on the end of the ferret line. No waiting until she turned up, no lying listening and digging down to the odd rabbit which would not bolt: the Squire and I were out for sport and he was prepared to leave his keepers to rabbit thoroughly, digging out everything which refused to bolt. Besides, it would have been a great pity to disturb the little buries out in the middle of open parkland, because they did provide refuge so precarious that there was always some quick sport.

It is surprising, in retrospect, how many rabbits we caught. Thirty in a day was by no means exceptional, and the Squire made shooting them look so easy that I took it for granted that he would not miss unless something went wrong. Experience taught me much later just how exceptional a shot he was. Few things are more difficult to hit than a rabbit on his way home, zigzagging through his tumps and tussocks of rushy parkland, out of sight behind clumps of rush as often as he is in view. But a gun came as naturally to his hand as a pen to a bank clerk, and he developed a wonderful sort of sixth sense which would predict in which direction the next swerve would be. Plenty of shots, far better than average, would not have hit one in four.

We always arrived back at the Hall about a quarter to one. Mick had to be deposited in one of an immense range of loose boxes which lined three sides of the stable quadrangle, and we went into the great front hall. This was floored in large stone flags, and displayed cannons and suits of armour, a stuffed albatross and literally hundreds of foxes' brushes. My nursery rhymes and stories had taught me to think of foxes as 'red'. These brushes were of every imaginable hue, from quite light yellow, through reds and browns and duns and greys, to black. One of the best naturalists I know—and quite the best professional terrier man—claims to know most of the individual foxes in his country by sight, and to be able to predict where any particular one will make for. Lots of very good countrymen put the claim as boastful bluff, but if they saw those Hilton brushes, they would understand that it was probably no more difficult than distinguishing by name the hounds in the pack that hunted them.

But the place I liked best was the Squire's study. It was quite small, long and narrow, at the side of the front door, off the hall. The butler always put me there to wait when I arrived in the morning, and we went there for a few minutes before lunch. It had all the things a lad or a countryman could want. Otters' masks, each telling the story of some hunt of special note that ended in a victory for the Squire, who had once been Master of Otterhounds; sporting prints of hunting and shooting, coursing and hawking; hunting horns and riding crops; gun cases and cleaning rods and shelf upon shelf of sporting and country and natural history books. One window looked over the lawn to the park, the view that had captured my imagination years before; and the other across the wide moat to the tower on a hill in the park, commemorating a victory of Admiral Vernon at Puerto Bello a century or so before. And locked in a cupboard, decently clad in a green baize bag, was Jack of Hilton. I never saw him for the next twenty-five years, and I was told that only male members of the Vernon family ever set eyes on him. He was a little bronze figure, used four or five hundred years ago in a feudal rite, but many centuries older than that, cast, originally, as if surprised in the midst of some sex orgy of obviously phallic origin.

Often, when I arrived with my ferrets and my dog, the Squire would send word that he could not come and that I was to carry on myself but be back at the house for lunch. I enjoyed these days best of all, for Mick was not on his lead and I did not trouble if he did run yowking after the odd rabbit or so. We would wander off into the park, out of sight of the house, and sit silent and still for a while, just inside one of the little woods, to watch what happened. I saw jays and magpies that had so far eluded the keepers. Several times a fox would slide silently across the rides and sometimes into the open, and kingfishers would fly from a chain of pools to the moat. Those brief, silent moments imprinted on my mind a longing to be able to sit and watch, when and where I wanted, a longing that has haunted me for the rest of my life and given me some of my happiest moments.

But the interludes were inevitably brief. Mick did not share my patience and was ever anxious to get on with the job in hand. I used to take with me about a dozen purse nets, nets of strong, fine twine that would cover a circle about two feet across. There was a brass ring at each end, and a cord was threaded roung the edge of the net through one ring and fastened to the other. The ends of the cord were fastened to a steel-wire stake about as thick as a pencil.

The idea was to open the net and spread it over a rabbit hole, driving the stake into the ground at the end of the cord. When a rabbit bounced out of a hole, hitting the centre of the net, the peg held fast and the net was drawn up, like a purse, on its cord, enclosing the rabbit a prisoner in the bag it formed.

Set with skill, purse nets are even more deadly than the

Squire's gun. The great thing is to approach into the wind, so that human stench drifts away from the holes, instead of down them as a grim warning. Stealth and silence, and great care never to walk over the holes, complete the deception. The ferret was put down, and the rabbits which bolted got no further than the entangling nets, except those clever or lucky enough to choose holes I had not noticed, or that were so placed that I should have had to blunder across other holes to reach them and would have warned all the rabbits in the bury that it was probably safer to stay down and meet fate at the fangs of the ferret. Mick was adept at taking care of these holes. He did not flinch when a rabbit bounced out to be brought up sharp in a net. Instead he crouched shivering, ears cocked, ready to 'field' anything that slipped through a hole otherwise unguarded.

Rabbits weigh about three and a half pounds each, and I could not carry many in addition to my ferret box and net bag. So I was told to hang them, light bellies outwards, on the corner posts of the little woods and shrubberies dotted all over the park, so that the keepers could see them easily and collect them when I was gone.

When I got back to lunch, I joined the Squire and Mrs Vernon in the dining-room. The windows looked out across the moat, and the meal was presided over by a statue which watched us from the alcove with unseeing, cold stone eyes. He used to worry me as a child, and I never liked him until, years after, I went into the room and found my host's granddaughter had draped a serviette over his outstretched arm, as if he were a dumb waiter. That piece of folded white cloth had stripped him of pomposity.

Although I was shy and gauche, the charm of those lunches melted my reserve. Gastronomically they were not elaborate, for the family seemed to me to live almost exclusively on shepherd's pie and mince, which I found rather dull. But the Squire and his lady talked gravely to me as if I had been their equal. Their families had been born and bred country folk

48

for centuries and they regarded their intimate knowledge of country lore as a perfectly normal social grace. We talked of game birds and vermin, and song birds and poachers and famous hunts. I heard of how the family had bred Diomed, the first winner of the Derby; of eccentrics and soldiers; and above all, of sportsmen and naturalists. On those days when I was rabbiting alone with Mick, I usually went back to tea as well, and one memorable day the Squire asked casually if I had had a good day and how many I had caught.

'Thirty-six, Sir,' I replied, doing what I could to look unconcerned.

'Good God,' he cried, 'that's more than my keepers kill. Wait until I tell them tomorrow that a chit of a child comes here rabbiting and does better than they do.'

It was not as simple as that, of course. They had to work the big buries, clearing them and digging out any that did not bolt. So much of their time was dissipated in catching the few awkward customers. I, on the other hand, could pick and choose where I tried, and as soon as I got into trouble, I simply pulled my little line ferret off and went to try elsewhere. But I do not imagine I was too popular with them the next morning when their master quoted my example, and sent them to collect rabbits, which I had hung in couples, belly outwards to be conspicuous, on fence posts all over the park.

If Mick made me friends among country folk wherever we went, he made me one enemy too: the head keeper at Hilton.

One day I was rabbiting some small buries right in the open when a stoat bolted instead of a rabbit. I always think a stoat, in a hurry, looks bigger and lower and much faster than it is. The white of its chest and belly melts into the ground, and the characteristic undulation, back arched and belly a hand breadth from the ground, melts into a furry red projectile, black of eye, tailtip and heart, as it streaks for safety.

All the same a stoat, even in a hurry, is not as fast as it looks. Mick streaked off in pursuit, overtaking it half a length with every stride he took. The end looked inevitable, until he stooped to pick it up in his vice of a grip and found he was biting thin air. At the last split second the stoat ducked to one side and the terrier missed it just as a greyhound so often misses a jinking hare. Again and again he caught up and struck, but every time he missed by the thickness of a skin. The air stank of pungent musk, and each time the dog's teeth clicked within touching distance; the frightened stoat chattered and the dog let out shrill yelps of bloodthirsty excitement. But with each attack and escape, the stoat made a few yards' ground toward a bury it was aiming for out in the open.

The squeals of the dog and my shouts of advice and encouragement echoed from Burn's Wood, until the inevitable happened and Hannam, the head keeper, heard us. Thinking it was poachers, he rushed from his cottage, brandishing his gun, and ran towards us.

When he saw who it was, he realized I had his employer's permission to be there; but he was furious about the noise, lest it scare his pheasants; the stoat was too near the dog for him to risk taking a pot at it; and the matter was only settled when it got to ground safely. There was silence for a while. Mick had his head so far down the hole, gulping down the intoxicating scent of thoroughly frightened stoat, that he was silent except for his breathing.

Hannam asked what I was going to do next.

'Put the ferret in and bolt it for the dog again,' I said.

He nearly had a fit. He had just seen for himself that the dog was no match for the stoat's agility, and he was of the opinion that the next goal would be the wood, where we certainly would not see it again. At the moment, on the other hand, there was no danger of escape, because the quarry was safely to ground in another small hole, from which it could either be dug or bolted by the ferret.

Any shooting man regards it as a criticism of his keeper if he sees a stoat at large in his preserves—and this was within two hundred yards of the keeper's house. It was not unnatural, therefore, that Hannam should be insistent that I put my dog on a lead so that he could make certain of shooting it when it was ejected. Indeed he went further than that. He wanted to block the entrances of the holes and fetch an assistant, to make certainty doubly sure, and wait until I had gone off on my rabbiting before finishing off my job.

I was also quite an insistent child. My ferret had found the stoat and bolted it; my dog had hunted it, if so far unsuccessfully, and I regarded it as my quarry, to be given the same chance as any other beast of the chase, and was in no mood to allow the keeper to slaughter it as vermin and take the credit for destroying it by hanging it on his gibbet with his crows and magpies and cat's tails.

So I told him, very politely, that I was in the middle of a hunt, that I was going to put my ferret in again to give Mick another chance, and that, if we lost it, it would be available for Hannam another day.

In the centre of great estates in those days, keepers were a law unto themselves and the word of a head keeper carried absolute authority. It was bad enough that his employer should invite some callow boy to catch rabbits, and worse that he should be told to go where he liked, except the big woodlands, accompanied by a yapping mongrel. This refusal to shorten the odds against a hunted stoat to the point of certainty was quite intolerable. Mick and I were enough to start a mutiny, and I believe we might have been reported forthwith to the Squire if it had not been for the risk that he might have replied that the matter would not have arisen if vermin had been adequately controlled in the first place.

So we glowered at each other in silence, each trying to win supremacy of will power; but the keeper was at a disadvantage. A lifetime of service had taught him to be courteous to his master's visitors—whether he liked them or not. In his philosophy it was guests and not customers who were always right. I suffered no such delusions. An only child, not particularly happy at home, I was growing up self-sufficient and well able to take care of myself, with skin thick enough to get me, unscathed, through all sorts of abrasive situations. It was not that I was insensitive, but that I simply did not mind very much that people thought me unconventional.

I won. I took my ferret from her bag again, made Mick crouch five yards or so from the hole, to avoid the danger of driving the stoat back underground to mix things with the ferret, and crept cautiously to the hole the dog had marked. Almost before the ferret's tail had disappeared down one hole, the stoat shot out of another and streaked for the woodland on what, to it, must have been the horizon. This time Mick made no mistake. As if he sensed his hostile audience, he made a dive and flicked the stoat, somersaulting, about ten feet into the air. Many dogs will not tackle stoats or weasels, not so much because of their bite, though that is fierce and venomous enough, but because of their stench. Stimulated by pain or fear, the musk gland near their anus secretes an almost tangible pong. If it gets on hands or clothes it hangs about for hours, and a sensitive nose can detect it for days. No wonder dogs don't like mouthing it. So Mick held it the minimum of time. A bite, a flick and he waited for it to land. Almost before it touched down, long before it had a chance to run, he had flicked it up again and next time it came down limp and dead.

It is surprising, the difference in effect between a live and dead stoat on a keeper's temper. Hannam was almost gushing in his praise of my dog, he went so far as to tell me of two good rabbit buries I had not discovered (though, by coincidence, they were as far as they could be from his pheasant coverts), and we parted, superficially at least, good friends. On the whole, I have always found more in common with individualists, the solitary chaps, who prowl deep in the countryside, a law unto themselves, than I have with the keepers who would constrict their activities. And the dogs without pedigree, good, useful working dogs, are certainly a most fruitful source of introduction to people who do not rate convention highly.

3. The Bodyguard

Mick was my constant companion during holidays from school and the whole of my formative years. He slept in an old box ottoman in my bedroom, he lay at my feet the whole time I was in the house and followed me like a shadow when I moved outside. His broad, bull terrier head was rather ugly, and he was a copy-book example of the idea that owners and dogs are often alike.

The fun we had together made the constriction and discipline of boarding-school the more unbearable. My dislike for most of the masters was mutual, I thought organized games dull and pointless and had little in common with most of my schoolfellows, who took easily to communal life.

Thorn was the one bright spot, and I did not meet him socially until I had been at my public school for about two terms. Then I was told—and I gathered that it was some sort of honour—that I had been appointed 'doul' to the head boy of my house. The school to which I went called fags 'douls', and a 'doul's' duty was rather like that of an unpaid, overworked cross between a batman and a valet. When I was not fetching or carrying or cleaning shoes or O.T.C. buttons or brewing tea or coffee or shopping, I was pressing trousers or washing rugger shorts for the senior boy to whom I had been allotted. There was no sort of payment if I was efficient, but if something was not done at all or not done well enough, I was beaten. The intellectual socialists of the post-war era would disapprove of any human soul being so much at the beck and call of another, particularly as the only reward was the negative one of escaping punishment only if a high enough standard of efficiency was attained. In point of fact I had no great objection because it meant that I always had an excuse to avoid group activities, which I disliked even more. There simply was not time. My job was the lesser of two evils.

The one part that I actively enjoyed was connected with Thorn. Thorn was the Headmaster's dog, and one of my duties was to find him every evening and take him to the Headmaster's study for the night. He was a large dog: to a small boy he was a very large dog. Marked like an Airedale, he had the coat of a collie, longer and less wiry than the harsh Airedale hairs.

But in size he was larger than either, and must have weighed nearer eighty pounds than seventy. I had seen him about for two terms, but nobody took too many liberties with him. He was an independent chap and would have had 360 masters if he had done the bidding of every boy in the school. So he ignored the commands of all with a strict impartiality. But one thing about him had caught my imagination. There was in the garden an ancient, spreading mulberry tree, the lowest branch of which was about six feet from the ground. There was not a shred of bark on its underside, and the grass around was worn bare as concrete, and padded nearly as hard.

Thorn, who had a monumental hatred of cats, had once 'treed' one here, pulled it down as it almost got to safety, and settled its account. It seemed that its ghost lived on, because, on summer evenings, the great dog would suddenly stare up into the empty tree, see the shade of his cat and begin to jump and worry at the lowest branch. He had a hoarse, throaty bark, which got deeper as his eyes glazed with fury, and he would leap and leap until he frothed at the mouth, eventually to sink down exhausted, baulked a thousand times by the cat that he had only conquered once.

I had witnessed this ritual often in my first two terms, and had come to the objective conclusion that the dog must be a fool. I have never suffered fools gladly, and the first night it became my duty to collect him, I went in search with some impatience.

I found him lying full-stretch on the grass in the middle of the quadrangle, grass that was inviolate from any feet less august than a master's, except for missions as specific as mine.

'Come on, Thorn,' I said, 'good dog.'

Thorn did not move an eyelid. There were umpteen more jobs to be done before bed to preserve my bruised posterior from further affliction, and I was in no mood to mess about. Nor was I accustomed to dogs which did not do what they were told. Bending down, I caught hold of his collar and lugged him to his feet.

It was a painful mistake, of which I still bear the scar as evidence. With a roar he turned on me and caught me by the forearm, slashing it open as he got a grip. I punched him as hard as I could in the neck with my free hand, and he let go, standing facing me with teeth bared, snarling like a lion. I retired to examine my wounds. The top of the arm was not too bad, little more than bruised, but there was a good gash in the soft underside. Having seen dog-bites cauterized, I avoided the matron, washed it clean myself and got a friend to bind it up. But the task was still not completed. If I said I could not get Thorn in because he had bitten me, I would be sent to Matron, whose treatment would probably be more painful still. If I made no excuse, I would be beaten for inefficiency. The only way out was to collect him.

I popped down to the kitchens, deserted at that time of evening, and took a handful of sliced meat.

'Good dog, Thorn,' I said, 'catch.'

A couple of pieces and he followed like a lamb back to my study. Like a lamb to the slaughter.

I shut the door and got a rugger bootlace out of the cupboard.

'Good dog, Thorn,' I said, as I stroked him, slipping a noose over his muzzle, as a veterinary surgeon does to a patient.

In a trice it was tied to his collar, and he was muzzled irrevocably. Then I showed him who was boss. I started with an O.T.C. officer's cane and laid in with all my might. Time and again he came at me in impotent fury, making no sound but muffled growls, because his jaws were tied too tight. I admired his guts, but once started, I had to carry on until he submitted, or he would have attacked like a demon the moment he got free. At last he gave in. I took off his muzzle and ordered him to heel. He followed me like a shadow to his master's study.

I never had to hit him again, and for the next three years we were the firmest of friends. Indeed he saved me from a good deal of bullying. There were two other people in our study besides the boy I 'douled' for. One of the others was three years older than me, and his only claim to distinction was a relationship to a bishop. All his anecdotes began 'My uncle the bishop'—a skeleton I would have kept in my cupboard. Because he was bigger than I was, he tried to extort by force the sort of services he could have claimed had I been his 'doul' too. Thorn and I had by now established our relative strengths—and there was no doubt at all who was boss. So, at the next outrageous request, I called Thorn, held him firmly by the collar and trod gently on his front foot. The immediate reflex reaction was a fearsome, snarling roar.

'Get to him, Thorn,' I said, and pressed a bit harder.

Then, above his roars, I shouted that if there was one spot more trouble from my big, hulking room-mate, I would set the dog on him. He didn't know enough about dogs to see that it was not he but I who was the object of the snarls, and word went round that the great dog was devoted to me and would tear to pieces anyone who so much as raised a finger. I was never bullied again.

But Thorn had more pleasant uses. The one time we were allowed off school premises was Sunday afternoon. There were a lot of sluggish brooks in the area, wandering between willows, through the meadows. Thorn, who had by now accepted me entirely, took to joining me on these Sunday walks, and I soon discovered that he had a marvellous nose. The banks of the brooks were riddled with ratholes, both common rats and water voles, and Thorn tested them as we walked along, as Mick would have done at home. I found a thin steel bar, about the size of a walking-stick, and when Thorn marked, I would plunge this into the bank and rock it to and fro. The story of rats leaving sinking ships is not far-fetched. They are very sensitive to unknown, unassessable danger and will often leave a bury in a body, if it is possible to produce earth tremors and a feeling of great insecurity by rocking a steel bar in soft earth near them. They used to 'plop' into the water and usually make for the other bank, encouraged by a shower of stones from me. At first Thorn could not see them until they emerged, although it was surprising how many he caught. But with experience, he could follow them with his eyes under the surface, and he would plunge his head under water to catch them as they swam. Once the dog knows what is going on, it is one of the most amusing ways of ratting. No waiting for ferrets, but good sharp fun, as long as there are tenanted holes. Thorn became an adept at pin-pointing where they were lying, and I got quite good at shoving my steel bar right in amongst them.

One by-product of the sport was accidental. In some of the fields there were a number of pit holes fed by the brooks, and very often Thorn would flush a water-hen off these. Usually it would fly about two hundred yards, and it needed little encouragement to get him in pursuit. It would get into thick cover, brambles or rushes, but he would keep working at it until it had to take to wing again. The bird's objective was to get to a sheet of water too large for the dog to flush it again, but there were not many pools, and our tactics were always to drive away from them. As the bird tired each flight became shorter than the last, and Thorn occasionally caught one in the end. It was quite a sporting chase, with odds on the quarry, and it had the immense compensation that we could eat the victim. I would skin and gut it on the spot, to avoid leaving too much evidence about at school, and take it back wrapped in my handkerchief. On two nights a week we were allowed to 'brew' in our studies. That is to say, we could use a spirit stove to boil water for coffee, and cook sausages and bacon in a frying pan. Anyone who experienced the squalor of pre-war boarding-school food will understand that the effort was well worth it.

When Thorn and I had had a successful hunt, we were far above plebeian sausage and bacon. We had a bird. And I mean 'we'. I pinched butter to baste it from the dining-hall, and used a biscuit-tin over my spirit stove as an oven. A packet of potato crisps completed the feast, and by the standards of school cooking it was a feast indeed. Thorn would sit by me, eating the ribs and neck and giblets, and we were the envy of all who savoured the wonderful gamey smell of our cooking. There were plenty of boys who coveted the crumbs which fell from 'my' dog's table. I am certain Thorn would agree that the one hiding he got, to establish our relative levels, was well worth it for all the sport we had afterwards, and every time I see the scar he has left on my arm, it evokes the few happy memories I have of school.

4. Fighting Dogs

By the time I left school at seventeen, I had two burning ambitions. One was to own a bull terrier and the other was to own a whippet.

To us, in Staffordshire, there was only one kind of bull terrier—the 'Stafford'. At that time it was not recognized as a breed by the Kennel Club, who only acknowledged 'English' Bull Terriers, the white, pig-faced, rather clumsy creatures evolved by Hinks in Birmingham nearly a century before. Many of them were deaf, in common with some other white dogs, and there was a movement afoot to breed 'coloured' English Bull Terriers, including some with the brindle and fawn markings of Staffords. But the fact remains, English Bull Terriers were show dogs, and ours, Staffords, were bred for work—the very specialized, brutal work of fighting each other in the dog pits.

Whippets were not recognized by the Kennel Club either. Or not the sort of whippet I wanted. My father had an industrial practice, and a great many of his patients were coal miners and ironworkers who still kept fighting cocks and bull terriers to fight, and whippets and pigeons to race. I grew up to know a lot of the men well, and loved nothing better than to spend Sunday morning on a tour of their back yards, admiring their dogs and their birds and hearing their stories of great races and battles—which often ended in a battle of owners as well.

For this reason it was not considered 'respectable' to keep 'a cock' or 'a dog', which were very specific terms in my youth. Any fowl that was not pure game, bred from stock which had been 'tried in the pit', was a 'muck hill', and any dog, however highly prized by the people who haunt dog shows, was 'a cur' if it was neither whippet nor pit dog. Coming from a 'respectable' household, I was told that I could not have a bull terrier until I was earning money to pay for the damage it did; and there would be no 'poacher's' dogs in the household either.

The first week's wages I ever earned, in an engineering works at Bilston, was forty-five shillings. I spent thirty shillings of it on Grip, my first bull terrier. At five weeks old he was pot-bellied with worms, and anything but promising. The bitch which bred him belonged to a chap in the factory toolroom, and the dog which begot him was said to have won some redoubtable battles. There was no pedigree and no proof. Fame of such dogs was spread by word of mouth and they had no highfalutin' Kennel names, like show dogs have. They were Arblaster's Mick or Timmington's Floss—and everyone knew that chaps like them didn't keep rubbish, or stuff that wasn't game.

Dog fighting had been illegal since 1837. It had not stopped, but penalties grew progressively tougher for those who were caught, until it finally died in the 1940s.

It was not as easy to get convictions for dog fighting as it was for cock fighting. There has always been a certain glamour about game fowl, and devotees of the sport come from every walk of life, from belted earls to Black Country colliers. Indeed, there have been two fairly recent prosecutions, on a large scale, for cock fighting, one just before the war and one in the 1950s. In both cases the cockers 'asked for it', because they grew so bold as to become foolhardy.

Indeed they sent their birds to one 'main' by rail. A game-cock has a most characteristic crow, and it is not surprising that eyebrows were raised at the number of baskets emitting martial music which arrived at one little Cheshire station. Authority—or a team of authorities—hid overnight, waited until battle had commenced with a vengeance, and collared the lot. The occupations of the captives ranged from miner to vet, from spinster to factory owner.

The dog men were far more cagey. It was a sport of working men, and on the whole pretty rough working men at that. The number of men at a fight was rarely more than four or five, they never fought at the same place twice—and they chose some pretty unlikely places too. I know of fights in a railway truck, a bedroom 'cellar', hollows in disused pit banks and even a chapel on Saturday night—and it would be difficult to conceive a more unlikely place than that. Finally, if trouble with the police did blow up, no body of men can stick closer and say less than a bunch of tough Black Country chainmakers and colliers.

The history of dogs bred specifically to fight goes back to the bull-baiting days of last century. At one time bull-baiting had been a lawful, even compulsory, pastime with a strictly utilitarian objective. Men have long believed—and I think correctly—that meat from an animal which has died after recent exertion is more tender than it would otherwise be. A hare that has been coursed is always deemed superior to flesh from a shot hare. The whole carcass is flushed and cleansed, the theory has it, by blood purged clean by effort. So a bull that has died defending himself from a succession of bulldogs, each bent on 'pinning' him with a vice-like grip of his tender cheek or nose, was thought to be less tough than he would have been without the enforced exercise. In medieval times it was illegal to kill a bull that had not been baited, and the owner of the bull was obliged to advertise the fact so that the locals could attend the last grim rites. This had the advantage that, since everyone knew when a bull was to be killed, it was extremely difficult to palm off bull meat on the unwary as prime beef.

A very special breed of dog was produced for baiting, more like a modern bull terrier than a present-day bulldog. Broad-chested and powerful, nostrils laid well back, so that it did not choke when it did catch hold, but much longer on the leg and more agile than the wheezing snufflers that are described on their pedigrees as bulldogs, although they are mere carica-tures of the real thing. The oil-painting over my fireplace of a working bulldog 150 years ago shows him to be taller and more racy than a show bull terrier. His snout is not so very much shorter, and he has a fine whip tail like a bull terrier, instead of the modern squiggle that culminates the deformities of modern bulldogs.

Such working dogs became obsolete in the first half of last century, and the breed became the plaything of people who showed their dogs but did not use them. In 1825 an act was passed to prohibit bull-baiting, not so much because of its cruelty as because of the disorderly crowds it attracted. The cholera epidemic which devastated Bilston was spread by the mob which converged for the orgies of the annual wakes. So Staffordshire ironworkers evolved another breed for their amusement. They crossed the working bulldogs of the day with various types of terrier.

The larger dogs they produced were the result of a cross between bulldog and English white terrier, which became extinct, as a breed, shortly after the turn of the century. It was a strong, agile, reachy dog, and the cross produced bull-and-terriers, as they were known, agile as weasels, staunch as bull-dogs and as fond of fighting as their masters.

These dogs were used for organized dog fights and matched against each other by weight, and very specialized rules were evolved. Smaller terriers, the little black-and-tan of Man-chester, tiny Yorkshire terriers and any other little dog that was game, were used both to cross with these larger bull-and-terriers and with the smaller bulldogs which had produced them. These little dogs were used in rat pits, where they were either matched against each other to kill a specified number of rats in a given time, or they were given a set time and had to kill as many rats as they could within that time.

Neither sport had quite died out when I was a boy. There was still no recognized type of Stafford. The Walsall dogs were fairly tall and reachy, fighting down to their opponents. Within four miles, in the Darlaston area, they had little dogs of around twenty to twenty-four pounds, eight or ten pounds lighter than the Walsall dogs; while in the chainmaking area, although the dogs were as heavy as Walsall dogs, they were shorter and thicker, bearing far more resemblance to the bull-dogs that sired their forebears. The different types were just a matter of choice. If an individual dog of any type was invincible, he would be used for a spell at stud and fashion would copy his profile.

Although I had been brought up amongst the dog men, they never talked to me about their sport while I was still a child. Oddly enough, I came into contact with many of them through the cockfighters who were captured in Cumberland just before the war. The man who had been responsible for their conviction had spent months plotting their downfall. Most of the 'cockers' will talk about their sport to a stranger, though they are naturally shy of showing him anything in-criminating; so that it is not really difficult to discover who keeps birds for use as well as ornament. The difficulty is catching them.

In this case, the architect of their downfall called at the home of a number of them, saying how keen he was on 'birds'. He ingratiated himself by referring, in familiar terms, to the hosts and their birds that he had visited previously, and each was lulled into a false sense of security because he assumed that his visitor was genuinely a friend of people he knew and respected. Eventually the ploy worked so well that he was allowed to join them at a main, where he arranged for their exposure and capture.

Old Pat, a patient of my father, was one of the last of the professional cock setters. That is to say that he would handle someone else's bird during its battle in the pit. It was a very skilled occupation, and the old man was known and liked by devotees all over the country. Only the fact that he happened to be smitten down with flu at the time prevented him from being caught with the rest in Cumberland.

When it was all over, the man who had engineered so wholesale a capture was not unnaturally jubilant. He gave it out that his next objective was the dog men and that he should go to Staffordshire as General in the campaign against them. So the game fowl men wrote to my old friend, who was a miner by profession though a cocker by inclination, and asked him to contact the dog men and warn them of the threat; and he came to my house and asked me to take him round in the car.

We went over to Cradley Heath, where we called at The Old Cross Guns in the centre of the town.

If you went today you might find it full of whippet men, but before the war there were almost as many bull terriers there as customers, though nobody ever referred to them as anything but 'dogs'. If a stranger walked in the hubbub ceased, except for the throaty snarl of dogs kept just out of each other's reach by their short slips and wide collars. All eyes would turn on the newcomer, and the silence was such that every word he spoke seemed to reverberate round the whole bar, until at last it was strangled by the impenetrable pall of smoke. It took a thick-skinned man to finish his pint. Very few stayed for a second.

But nobody took any notice of me, because it was accepted that Pat would take in nobody who was not 'all right'. Grip, my puny bull terrier pup, had grown into a lithe, rather reachy, Walsall-type dog, and I took him along to see what the dog men of that part of the world would think of him. If Pat was regarded as the perfect chaperon for a young man, there was no doubt that Grip was the perfect introduction.

Joe, the landlord, eyed him up and down, and came over and handled him. No Black Countryman ever trusts the evidence of his eyes without the tactile confirmation of his sensitive hands. He eased him clear of the ground to assess his weight more accurately; he tried the texture of muscle and loin and shoulder and thigh; he slid the dog's lips up over the gums, to be certain his mouth was neither overshot nor undershot, but level.

'How's he bred?' he asked. 'Will he go?'

I told him I had never tried, and that I kept him for ratting.

'He looks to me as if he'd go,' he said. 'I've got an old dog down the cellar. Bring him down to try for five minutes while there's a row up here.'

Nothing is more of a nuisance, when one is out ratting, than a dog which will leave its legitimate quarry to sail into the first dog it sees. I knew enough to be quite certain that he was bred from fighting stock, and once he tried it, he would rather fight than live. Besides, I was extremely fond of him, and hated the idea of getting either him, or the old dog down the cellar, hurt. I declined the offer firmly, saying that my friends all came out ratting on Sunday mornings (a slight exaggeration) and I did not want to risk getting him 'fast'. I was to find out later, by accident, just how wise my decision was. Grip lasted four years without ever fighting anything. It was a side of his character that had not yet developed, that first night at Joe's, and my firmness in declining the invitation to 'try' him allowed me over two years of peace, before he discovered what he was bred for.

When I would not play Joe lost interest. Most of the customers seemed either very big or very wiry: thick men or thin men, depending on how the heat of their work affected them, whether the sweat boiled out of them in quarts or whether they were pale and leathery, apparently impervious. Either way, they replaced the loss, or threatened loss, with pint after pint of beer, and as the evening went on the talk grew gruffer and deeper and broader, in colourful phrases, always describing some feat of courage by cock or man or dog, for that is all that seemed to interest them. From time to time an owner would grow careless, let his slip hang loose for an instant, so that his dog could take that vital pace nearer his neighbour.

There was not an instant's hesitation. The moment a dog discovered he was within reach of another dog, he dived right in. No growling or snarling, the blow came before the word. There was no immediate indication of what was going on. Dogs normally sat under the benches which lined the walls, in self-defence from the great hobnailed boots which cluttered the bar floor. When they started to fight, they fought silently, determined on destruction. It was as if a poltergeist was present in the room. Any vacant stools within yards spun off, apparently of their own volition; glasses were nudged from fingers and crashed from rocking tables. In their efforts to step clear of the canine whirlwind among their feet, several men toppled to the floor, their dogs escaping in the confusion, to join the fray.

It was easy to start two bull terriers fighting, two of the bull terriers of those days anyhow. The modern breed has become respectable, joined the Kennel Club and grown emasculated. They are harder to start and easier to stop than in my day, when nobody kept one that would not 'go'. In some pubs you would be chucked out for letting your dog fight. Not from Joe's. He always kept a good one or two and was interested to assess the 'form' of his customer's dogs, if they got together accidentally. Nobody really minded a couple getting together. They might curse over spilt beer or barked shins, but they were really as interested as Joe. I could see nothing but a flurry of wrestling bodies, convulsing as the dog with the master-hold heaved and shook to weaken his foe. But half the time I can't tell who is winning a boxing match because my eyes concentrate on the fighters more than on the fight. The customers at Joe's were different. They assessed every move with the eyes of experts: careless, as the contestants, of pain, they were obsessed with sheer technique.

'Come on, lads, break it up. You'll have the bloody coppers here.'

Joe did not need to tell them twice because they knew it was no bluff; but it was easier said than done, because genuine fighting dogs do not let go so easily. The first thing was to let one or other get a sound hold, so that it was possible to get a firm grip of them without thrusting heedless hands into the mêlée. Then it was possible to catch hold of whichever dog had the firmer grip. A hand each side of his neck, thumbs on the base of his skull, fingers so placed that they could squeeze the root of his tongue up to his throat.

The best dog in the world will let go quite soon if you choke him off with his own tongue. The thing to be certain about is that someone has got the other dog, so that he swings clear the instant his adversary lets go. If he is any good at all he will strike like an adder, for revenge, as soon as he is at liberty, and the most likely place for him to connect is on the other dog's neck, right on the knuckles and fingers which freed him.

More than a century ago dog fights were freely advertised, and round-by-round descriptions published in the sporting press. They are published in America now, and the dogs they use, American Pit Bull Terriers, are descended from the same stock as the Staffords were until the dog shows got hold of them.

Although strictly illegal last century, it was really the 1911 Cruelty to Animals Act which killed them. Instead of aiming to stop riotous assemblies, this Act made it illegal to bait any animals or cause them to fight: it set out to abolish cruelty. It did not have much effect before the Great War, because dog and cock fights were still held pretty openly among the pit banks and factories of the Black Country. After the War things tightened up a lot. Cocking was fairly easy, and still is, if you are not fool enough to invite more than a handful of folk you can trust, and you do not talk about it afterwards. During the last war I got some birds for a prominent Birmingham industrialist, and he and his friends used to while away the hours in air raid shelters with a quiet bit of cocking —and then talk about it in the club next day. It nearly caused their downfall, and attracted a lot of attention, which made the regulars lie low for some time. But you cannot put a bull terrier in your poacher's pocket; the neighbours are apt to miss him if he disappears, and notice if he gets cut up in a fight. The whole thing grew far harder to organize, so that by the 1950s there were no more than half a dozen men left who could handle a dog in the pit, and even they turned to whippet racing, when the sport revived; so that there is not any dog fighting done now, and I doubt if it would be possible to find any of the right sort of game dogs left.

Make no mistake, it takes a brave dog to win, and it is a good thing the game has died because it really was a viciously cruel sport, with almost as many wrangles as in dog racing.

The first thing was to get the dog fit. 'Well' they call it, in the fancy, which was somewhat of an understatement. He —or she, for bitches fought as gamely as dogs—had to be as strong as possible consistent with carrying no fat at all, or as thin as possible without losing strength, whichever way you looked at it. The only dogs I have ever seen carrying as little flesh as fighting dogs are the dogs they use for hound trailing in the Lake District. These run ten miles up and down a mountain in sweltering heat, which would give normal dogs heart failure or uremic fits. A fighting dog might fight and worry and be worried by a dog the same weight for sixty or more consecutive minutes, which is probably the most gruelling thing for mind and body that any breed of dog could be required to undergo.

Even out of training a fighting dog was never allowed to put on flesh. His diet consisted of first-class sound meat and eggs and toast, only sufficient to keep him strong. Two or three weeks before he was wanted for work he was given a purgative, to get him completely empty, and put on a sloppy diet, to bring him a pound or so below the weight at which he was matched to fight. This got him a little 'poor', or below condition, and he was given plenty of road work.

Road work meant exactly what it said. He was fitted with a wide collar, usually two inches wide, attached to a short slip, or lead, just long enough for him to stand comfortably below his trainer's hand. An assistant with another dog then walked two or three yards in front, and the dog in training was encouraged to try to catch up with it. As soon as he pulled, his front legs pawed the air an inch or more above the ground, and the whole of his weight was taken on his hind legs, with every muscle in loin and neck and back brought into play. Six to ten miles a day of this for two or three weeks would make every muscle stand out and ripple like an advertisement in a Naturist magazine. In passing, I would say that the trainer got pretty fit too. It was like going for a ten-mile walk with thirty-five or forty pounds pulling on one's arm.

For wind, as opposed to muscle, two methods were used. 'Ball work', plenty of ball work was essential. Most bull terriers love chasing a solid rubber ball, and by making it bounce, they could be encouraged to jump and twist and turn like fireworks; and when they had done that, they 'worked on the tyre'. All this consisted of was an ordinary motorcycle tyre suspended from a beam, often on a tension spring, so that its lower rim was about eighteen inches above the ground. It was quite irresistible to any bull terrier I ever saw. Swing it at him, set him on and encourage him, and he would seize the lowest part of the tyre. I suppose, when it flexed and the spring stretched, it felt as if it was alive. The dog shook it and backed away, still tugging. Again his front legs were lifted clear of the ground, but this time all the muscles were pulling in the opposite direction to the strain of road work. They loved it so much that I have seen dogs work at the tyre until they were literally ready to drop from sheer exhaustion, and a clever trainer knew just when to break off so that they were mad to rejoin battle the next time they saw it. Ten to fourteen days produced a dog as hard as whipcord and as fit as an Olympic runner. He was ready for the 'pit'.

A dog pit was usually about nine feet across, round or square, with a line marked, or 'scratched', across the centre. The dogs were weighed, and either would be disqualified if it scaled more than one pound over the weight at which the match was made. It was said that an ounce for a fighting cock, and a pound for a fighting dog, equalled a stone for a fighting man. Weighing was one of the first spheres of chicanery. One famous handler had a pair of steelyards which he was reputed to be able to make do anything but talk. His dog would show forty pounds when anything up to forty-two, while his opponent's weights read right. He knew the exact weight of his dog and would have been suspicious if it suddenly changed. In the absence of dead weights, it was common for a handler to weigh himself on a public weighing-machine, first alone and then carrying the dog in his arms. Subtraction gave the weight, but with no great accuracy; and spring balances were often worse.

After weighing, both dogs were washed in fresh milk, after which each setter had the privilege of 'tasting' his opponent's dog. He could lick or taste any part he thought might be doped, to satisfy himself all was well. It was not uncommon to put acid or strong alkali on the coat of one dog's neck and legs, to discourage his adversary from retaining a hold too long; and the only way to be sure that all was well was to 'taste' the opposing dog yourself.

When all was ready, each handler took an opposite corner of the pit, after tossing for which dog should 'scratch' or 'go across' first. When the referee gave the word, the dog to scratch was loosed and was expected to rush across the pit at his opponent, who was loosed in time to defend himself. Generally they started fighting, and neither could then be touched until both stopped and neither 'had a mouth on' or was biting the other. This normally only happened when they were compelled to stop for breath, and might well be forty or fifty minutes after they started.

When they broke off, either handler could pick his dog up, which constituted the end of the round. A minute was allowed to wash them down, after which it was the second dog's turn to go to scratch. The first dog to fail to go across in his turn lost the battle. This could be because he had had enough, was too weak or had died.

There was a great deal of ring craft for the handler to learn. He had to assess if his dog was still enjoying himself or was ready to pack it in. If there was any danger that he would not go across, he was better left as long as possible. Sometimes both dogs were too exhausted, in which case it would pay a handler to lift his dog, if it was not his turn next, and take him away unobtrusively. A very tired dog might not try to find him if he had not seen him taken away. Even a dead dog could win, for if it was his opponent's turn next, the rules laid down that he must go across and worry, even if he had killed his adversary in the last round. If he did not go, the dead dog was declared the winner.

The sport finally died out about ten years ago, and I knew several of the last of the dog-fighting fraternity well. I could not have watched a fight through without being physically sick, but I believe that was only because I was more imaginative than men who enjoyed it. With one exception, I do not think they were sadistic. Most of them loved fighting among themselves, they admired courage above all else, and they knew their dogs loved fighting and that it was impossible to make a coward dog fight. I do not think they were capable of conjuring up any picture of the anguish their superlatively brave dogs suffered, particularly the day after the fight.

Grip was my first bull terrier bred from fighting dogs, and Rebel my second. Neither of them were ever either matched or tried in the pit, although both took to fighting as naturally as a spaniel to the gun. I kept them for their company, because

72

I have always been intrigued by traditions that are passing, because they were the sources of introduction to a great many Black Countrymen I should not otherwise have known, and because no dog in the world is better at ratting.

It was necessary to keep an eye on old Grip or he would leave what he was doing for anything with a long coat. I was cycling along the canal tow-path with him one day, because I find it an excellent place to exercise dogs. There is no traffic to run over them, few people, and usually plenty of warning of other dogs, because it is possible to see so far along the level tow-path. It is also ideal for cycling because there are no hills. When I exercised Grip along the canal therefore, I could let him run loose and give him fairly hard exercise by keeping him going at a fair pace. He was completely steady to stock, so there was no worry about cattle in adjacent fields; he was all right with dogs with short coats, and with cats. His only hates were rats and shaggy dogs.

This started quite by accident. Every morning, without fail, a local collie came to the field behind our house to play with Grip. It was ideal exercise for them both, and they would rough-and-tumble for an hour or more, in the best of good spirits, until they were forced to lie down in panting exhaustion. One day, Grip got his dew-claw caught up in the collie's collar and broke it off, which he naturally found extremely painful.

He didn't stop to think, no process of reasoning whether it was by accident or design, on the part of his playmate, delayed his instinctive action for an instant. One moment he was a civilized house-dog, playing with a friend. The next, he had reverted to generations of fighting dogs. He turned on his friend in silent fury, getting a grip on his throat and shaking him like an old duster. It is this instinct to shake that is so devastating in fighting dogs. Sooner or later the whole mouthful is so crushed that no more damage would be done if it broke away—as it often did. They never let go—except to change to an even more lethal hold. They shake and worry

73

to kill, and some of them would go on shaking and worrying long after the life of their adversary was extinct.

Luckily I was there in time and was able to choke him off before much damage was done to the collie. But I was too late to prevent the damage to my dog. It was psychological and not physical. Thenceforth, whenever he saw a collie or a sheepdog, or a spaniel or a chow, it was as if the Bad Fairies had waved their magic wands. He waited for no introductions, nor tarried to see if they were dogs or bitches. All were alike to him, and he sailed straight in.

Perhaps the most convincing demonstration I saw of this was that day when I was exercising him along the canal bank. All seemed to be clear until we came under the bridge, and there, huddled with his fishing-rod out of the wind, was a man and his sheepdog. There was a flurry, and Grip had got a shoulder hold. They rolled over and over, the sheepdog lashing at his flanks with no effect at all. I couldn't get hold to choke him off, for the simple reason that his opponent's attention would simply have been transferred from Grip's flanks to my hands. So I took the only alternative I could see: I caught Grip by the tail and tipped them both into the canal.

It had the desired effect. The shock made him loose and they came up gasping—but separate. My triumph was short-lived. Instead of swimming to the bank, the bull terrier took another hold, this time of the neck, and started to shake again.

He was not much more than half the weight of his opponent, who was concentrating on keeping his head above water, so Grip spent most of his time submerged, and I seriously feared that he would drown and die still hanging on. When he did let go, almost in his extremity, they were both too weak to crawl up the bank, being weighed down by the water they had shipped; so that I had to lug the sheepdog out first, and then my own dog, who was still game to carry on and had to be restrained by his slip.

It isn't any use trying to thrash that sort of aggression out of a fighting dog, the pain simply makes him worse. So I never let him loose again except when I was certain there was no danger, and my success can be judged by the fact that he lived for nine years, had only about three fights with other people's dogs, and I was always able to part them before real damage was done.

He was not just a fighting machine. He was a wonderful house-dog and guard, never savage with people, although I had complete confidence that, had any intruder tried any rough stuff, and roused him, he would have been as implacable and effective in his hatred as with a four-footed foe. He was also one of the most intelligent dogs I ever had, and I shall always remember one incident, in particular, which gives the lie to any theory that dogs do not think but only act by instinct or reflex.

The summer-house at home was at one side of the tennis court, with a space of about nine inches between the corner of the building and the corner post of the wire-netting surrounding the court. A party of us were sitting just outside the summer-house, watching the game in progress and taking no particular notice of Grip, who was always keen on a bit of fuss and attention. He tired of his neglect, and being a natural extrovert, he determined to attract our attention. There was a branch, blown off by winter's gales, still lying on a flower-bed at the end of the court, and I happened to be watching when he noticed it. He knew from experience that, when he retrieved anything to hand, everyone said 'Good dog' and made much of him, so he squeezed between the post and summer-house to fetch the branch.

It was quite a large stick, six or eight feet long and as thick as a man's wrist. Sensibly, he picked it up by the centre, so that it balanced, and then he brought it towards us. Naturally enough, he stuck at the narrow gap, a few inches wide, with his two-yard burden. He shoved and wriggled to no avail, appreciated the situation, turned and set off round three sides of the tennis court, to carry it to us along a route unobstructed by narrow constrictions. That showed at least some power to think, but having gone only a few yards he stopped and re-traced his steps.

I watched him stop and think things out, and it was obvious that it had suddenly dawned on him that there was a quicker and easier way of getting his stick where he wanted it than carrying it through shrubs round three sides of the lawn. He brought it back to the narrow gap, put it down and came through without it. Then he turned round, poked his head through, caught hold of the very end and dragged easily through lengthwise what had defeated him askew. He got it on our side of the court, picked it up again by the centre and strutted for his applause like a *prima donna*. After that piece of constructive thinking, nobody will ever convince me that it is beyond the mental capacity of dogs to reason.

When Grip was about five an old fancier gave me Rebel, a bitch pup that I thought would be able to learn the tricks of the trade in plenty of time to follow him on. The lives of dogs are so relatively short, and the gap they leave when they do go so marked, that I find it far easier to have more than one. The void is not quite so absolute.

Despite the obvious difficulties of keeping a dog and bitch in the same house, I chose a bitch for the simple reason that Grip would never have consented to share his home with another male. As it turned out it made little difference.

At first, all was well. Staffords are wonderful with children or almost anything young and helpless. The fiercest fighting dog often will not kill a tame rabbit. So Grip and Rebel were a joy to watch. They played by the hour, and by the time Rebel was six months old, she was coming out ratting on Sunday mornings. I had begun again with Rebel at the point I had left off with my old half-bred, Mick. She took to the sport like an old hand. Her sire, O'Rooney, was a famous fighting dog, and the first rat which bit her nose sealed the fate, in her mind, of all rats. She and Grip both killed with one crunch, wasting no time on shaking; both of them killed over a thousand rats in a season and both over a hundred in a session. A hundred rats is quite a pile, a good wheelbarrow full, and about the only time one ever comes across so many together is when a rick is being threshed. When the corn is done and the rick is down to its straw bottom, the whole base heaves and quakes if it has really been infested. That is where a really game dog shines. He will shove his snout down and root about like a pig, probing out every hidden rat. The result, of course, is that it is impossible for him to avoid being bitten, and I have seen both Grip and Rebel come away from a rick with as many punctures in their faces as there are holes in a colander. The more they were bitten the more ruthless they became.

Ferreting and threshing were much like the old days with Hairy Kelly, but I had absorbed enough knowledge of the game to be adequate without more help. I always kept a fair number of ferrets in a large, open run, and I fed them on flesh. The extent of their exercise paddock made them almost as quick as the rats themselves, and the quality of their food gave them strength. But I had to keep a lot, simply because they never lasted long. We did so much ratting that it was inevitable they got cut-up a fair bit, and ferrets do not tolerate many hidings before they find other things better to do than venture down ratholes; and they will flatly refuse to go up to any rat that faces them. So it was vital to keep reinforcements to replace them.

We had some of the quickest and most lively sport at night. Rats come into the farm buildings when the corn is cut in the autumn, and usually start 'working' the ricks. For a week or so it is quite easy to hear them, an hour after dusk, rustling in the straw, and it is often possible to make them jump into the open by probing with a steel rod. Quite soon, however, they take up residence in some more or less impregnable fortress about the farm, and only venture out at night to feed.

My technique, if possible, was to wander round the farm buildings in daylight first and try to assess where the rats were and where they were feeding. Sometimes they might be lying in the complicated maze of drains that old farms have, or in buries round the duck pond, or under the scrap iron and obsolete farm implements that seem to accumulate in most rickyards. Roofs that had been insulated against heat loss by having felt nailed to the underside of rafters made a wonderful dormitory, and so did rucks of pig muck and the under side of wooden floors. It was easy for a trained eye to locate and assess the rat population, and simple to deduce where they were probably feeding.

It was quite a different proposition to forecast which way they would try to escape. The proof of that pudding lay in its eating, and we never expected great success during the first few visits. The great thing was to allow plenty of time after dusk before disturbing them, which gave a good excuse to enjoy a spot of hospitality in the farmhouse first. Then, at eight or nine o'clock on winter evenings, we would sally forth with the dogs, a powerful torch, a stick and an old sack.

It is wonderful how silently bull terriers can move when they realize the need. Normally they seem such boisterous, rumbustious dogs, bulldozing their way through thick and thin. Grip and Rebel, on the other hand, would pick their way around yard and farm buildings as delicately as a cat avoiding puddles. They had sensitive noses and would stop and listen outside each shed door, testing the air with their noses, their forefeet poised in query. If there was nothing of interest there, they would slide on like two shadows, but if a rat was feeding inside they seemed to be able to wind him, though the air was rank with pigs or heavy with the breath of oxen, and to hear him, however much grunting and trampling and rustling of straw there was within.

Ratting at night took at least two people as well as the dogs. We would creep up to the door, fling it open, and switch on the light if there was one, or our torch if not. The dogs swept round, chopping as they went any rats still in the open, and one of us stuffed a sack along the bottom of the door while the other watched for rats running up the corners of walls or woodwork of stalls, and dealt them a blow with his stick. In most sheds there is some cover. A trough or corn-bin, hay bales or nest boxes, where any rats we surprised took refuge if they could. As soon as the dogs had dealt with any trying to escape, or had lost them, they wheeled round to try for refuge. This time, they knew there was no need for silence and stealth. They knew, from experience, that a good deal of noise would often make any that had ducked into cover lie closer still, and when they located one behind a box or under a bale, they pranced round in excitement, begging us to come and bolt it.

So far as we were concerned there was no hurry. The main thing was to go round first, stuffing sacks or handfuls of straw into every likely crevice, blocking every way of escape we could. Then we went round systematically turning everything over that the dogs thought sheltered a rat.

It was a sporting sport in the sense that the odds were in favour of the quarry. There were always holes and drains and eaves where we lost them, and though we got wiser on each visit, the potential bag dwindled as we began to account for most of the rats on the farm. There were no astronomical bags: with one exception, the most we ever caught in an evening was thirty-five. But there was scope for action almost akin to gamekeeping.

Oddly enough, the biggest factor contributing to escape was lack of suitable cover. If ten rats were feeding in a cow-shed where there was nowhere for them to hide, they would be far more edgy than if there were hollows between the stalls, or a short drain where they could dive if danger threatened. Those that did not melt away before we arrived scattered in every direction when we did, and some had time to escape before the dogs had finished dealing with the first. So, quite deliberately, we tried to put some sort of artificial cover in every area where rats were in the habit of feeding. And we tried to block permanently all but two or three escape

79

holes, so sited that we could deal with them in seconds when we did arrive. In this way the sport was spread out, and we did not eject one rat until those already on foot had been accounted for. It was quite impracticable to use ferrets at night, because of the damage to poultry they might do if they got into a hole not known to us, and escaped in the darkness. Besides, if a ferret lay up we might be there till morning. But we bolted many a one from short drains and holes with a bucket of water, and if they were stubborn it was always worth fetching a bucket of hot from the house. Rats are wonderful swimmers, and if they know there is peril outside, they will almost drown before cold water ejects them. But warm water is something of which they have no experience. They are terribly afraid of the unknown, be it temperature or earth movement—as when they bolt because a bar is thrust into their bury, or because of a sudden stamping immediately overhead. The first drop of hot water will throw them into panic.

The one snag about ratting is jaundice. Rats are frightful carriers of this disease, which is very fatal to dogs. Things are better now that most puppies, when they are inoculated against distemper, are covered against jaundice too. But I do not know for how long the immunity lasts, and I still would not like to risk a dog of mine being bitten by a jaundiced rat, however recently he had been inoculated.

In the days when I had Grip and Rebel, they were not even inoculated, and killing as many rats as they did, it is obvious now that, in the end, it was almost inevitable that they should contract the disease that would eventually lead to their doom.

Before they did, however, they started to fight. They lay by the sitting-room fire one afternoon, when I was due home from work, and, unfortunately, the door was a few inches ajar and opened into the room. When they heard the car arrive, they got up simultaneously and made a rush to greet me, both arriving at the door at precisely the same instant. Naturally, as they shoved and hustled, the door was pushed further shut, crushing them both against each other and against the jamb. The story of Grip and the collie was repeated, and each took it as a personal slight from the other. They forgot all about me and settled down to fight in earnest.

I was on the scene within seconds, and managed to part them before they had done each other more than superficial mischief. But the walls, which were newly decorated, were spattered with blood, and so was the carpet and furniture. By far the most serious result, however, was that they could never be trusted alone together again.

The mechanics of keeping two house-dogs apart are more complicated than one might imagine. Either they have to be chained up—a practice common amongst Black Country folk, if they kept more than one game dog—or some door between them must always be latched. Always. It was almost like keeping in the house a lion which might eat a neighbour if the back door stood ajar for a few seconds. A telephone conversation or ring at the door-bell was all it needed.

The strain almost got my wife down. Her heart is soft, and she cannot bear the thought of anything being hurt, especially our own dogs; and it takes considerable physical strength to part two bull terriers who mean business. Indeed the only way for one person to do it is to wait until they are really stuck in, fasten a lead to the collar of whichever dog is pinned and tie the lead to the door-knob or a heavy piece of furniture. Then it is possible to choke the other off with some chance that his victim cannot lay hold as soon as he is freed. No job for a woman, even of Amazonian proportions: my wife would not have had a chance.

So, when Grip contracted jaundice at the age of nine, and began to waste away, we felt there were practical advantages, however fond we were of him.

Although we realized that jaundice was the ultimate cause of his death, or would have been had we not had him destroyed to spare him the last miseries, it did not dawn on us at the time that rats were the cause of the disease. I had tried and do try, any sport with dogs that I can, from beagling and otter hunting to watching setters find the grouse for hawks. But, apart perhaps from coursing, there is no sport, to my way of thinking, that can hold a candle to ratting. The result was that Rebel and I and the ferrets continued to go ratting whenever we could.

Just as Grip had introduced me to sportsmen all over the Black Country, Rebel was really my chief entrée into the farming community. She was a big, strong white bitch of about forty pounds, with a patch of fawn over one eye. The only dog I have ever seen which could kill a rat as quickly is a smooth lurcher, asleep on my hearthrug now, but I doubt if she would go on killing nearly so long as Rebel did or put up with half the punishment she received, if the rats needed 'winkling out'. Greyhounds are, in any case, noted for their prowess at killing rats.

With experience Rebel became a specialist, a real artist, and her fame spread far and wide. Indeed, I bathed in her reflected glory. Strangers, who had no idea of my name, would nudge each other and say, 'There goes the bloke what belongs that lemon-eyed bitch.'

With no Grip for her to fall out with, life at home lost its tensions. She was, to all else, a friendly, great-hearted soul, an ornament to be seen out with, and would probably have been a good guard in time of need. I say 'probably', because, though potentially effective as a guard, she was a poor house-dog, even accompanying the only burglar we ever had as he toured our house whilst we were out. An overdeveloped sense of hospitality, we thought.

In the end, however, her undoing was the same as Grip's. A friend had done a broadcast about the Birmingham City Salvage Department, and had discovered, during his re-searches, that there were a lot of rats there. So he told the Ratcatcher—who basked in some such title as Pest Destruction Officer—that he had a pal who loved a bit of ratting and had a good dog. 'Well, if he came here,' said the ratcatcher, 'the rats would chase his dog out of the building. There are as many as that.' My friend passed the message on, to which I replied that, if rats did make my dog turn tail, I would get another dog.

The upshot was a meeting one night in some little pub in the centre of Birmingham, somewhere at the back of the Salvage Department. We had a pint or so and then were taken 'to see the rats'. It was impossible to loose the dog because of the geography of the place. As an example of municipal engineering, I suppose it was a masterpiece—apart from the rats. It was a multi-storey building, and the refuse was tipped from lorries that collected it on to moving belts. These belts took it past rows of men, who sorted out rags or bones or other material which could be salvaged. At the end of the floor it simply tipped down to the next, where the process was repeated.

I never saw more rats in my life. They scurried in all directions and did not bother to do much more than get out of the way. There were mountains of waste waiting to be sorted or burned, and they had made great buries in these, like rabbit warrens; and they sat at the mouths of their holes, grooming or eating or fighting or making love, as the spirit moved them. Rebel was beside herself with excitement, but I dared not let her off her slip lest she should fall down one or more storeys while chasing a rat along the edge, or be caught up in the moving machinery. So we decided to have a 'quiet' walk round, keeping the dog on the slip, whilst our hosts accompanied us with air-rifles, to which they had fixed torches, so as to illuminate their targets.

A bull terrier slip is a very short lead, perhaps twelve or fourteen inches long. Her radius of activity was limited to this plus the length of my arm, as I bent down to allow her as much scope as possible. Even so, she killed no fewer than twenty-five rats on a tour of the building lasting perhaps a quarter of an hour. If it had been safe to have loosed her, I do not doubt that she could have quadrupled the figure and

83

equalled or passed her 'record' when threshing. Our hosts with the air-rifles did even better. They shot sixty-five, mostly sitting watching us from the false security at the mouths of their holes. The range was not very great, perhaps seven to ten yards, but I had not realized how deadly an air-rifle can be to rats. There was just a dull 'plop', and a rat would roll from his perch and lie twitching in death at the foot of the slope. Even before he had finally convulsed into immobility, his brothers and cousins began to eat him.

I shall never forget the stench when I got home. In the excitement and turmoil at the City Salvage Department I had forgotten it after the first few minutes. It crept up on me insidiously in the car on the way back, and I thought it was Rebel and that I should have to bath her before she could settle for the night on her chair in the kitchen. Then it dawned on me that I smelt quite as bad. It was not a wholesome smell, in the sense that farmyard manure is. It was not even an animal smell, however unpleasant, like the smell given off by creatures when they are not well. It was the musty stench of putrefaction, and I felt defiled.

Luckily I had gone in my oldest clothes, so I stripped naked in the yard and left them in a pile to be soaked in petrol and burnt the next morning. I left the old bitch in the stable while I went in the house for a bath and to wash my stinking hair. The stuff clung to everything like stale cigar smoke. Then I bathed the dog and went to bed. How people can be persuaded to work in such an atmosphere of filth is quite beyond my comprehension. Perhaps there have been advances in methods of keeping rats at bay since the 1940s, but I marvelled, at the time, that rats travelling from the Salvage Department to adjacent food shops and markets, in the city centre, did not spread waves of foul disease.

In any case, I always believed that one night's ratting sealed the fate of my old dog. In years she was only seven, but she started to go downhill, contracting a form of jaundice, and within a few weeks she was dead.

Author's Dinah. A whippet-lurcher, produced by crossing pure whippet dog with whippet/terrier bitch. (*Derek Johnson*)

An old-fashion
start — now ille
—where the slip
throws the dog
land in his stride
full speed. (*D*
Johnson)

A modern st
where the dog
simply released
pushes himself
with both hind f
(*Derek Johnson*)

(*Above*) The race. A bad start. The pistol has fired, but no dog is yet on the move.

(*Below*) A good start. The pistol has cracked, and three out of four dogs are already on their way. (*Derek Johnson*)

Bert Gripton, the terrier man, with a bunch of the right sort of working terrier
(Derek Johnson)

The end of the dig. The terrier keeps just out of reach and 'bays' or 'speaks' to the fox, to keep him where he is and to let his master know where he and his quarry are. (*Derek Johnson*)

Bert Gripton handles the fox, which is alive and unharmed. (*Derek Johnson*)

Author's Gypsy. A lurcher, produced by crossing half-bred deerhound and thoroughbred coursing grey-hound. (*Derek Johnson*)

Author's lurcher bitches Amber and Gypsy in action close on their hare. (*Derek Johnson*)

The loss of two brave dogs before their time, both from diseases they caught from rats, sickened me, and I determined to change my sport to something less lethal to my dogs. In any case, my wife and I decided that we would never keep a bull terrier again. The 'real thing', bred from fighting dogs, was really more trouble and responsibility than it was worth. Sooner or later, try as we might, we could no longer prevent it from fighting, and a dog fight of that sort is a very bloody business. The continual vigilance necessary to keep even our own dog and bitch from tearing each other's throats had seriously affected my wife's nerves, and the trouble was not worth it.

Meanwhile the dog show people had got hold of the breed and enfeebled it. They penalized dogs in the show-ring if they showed signs of being 'fast' or aggressive. They were fixing a stockier, bigger-headed type which looked the part of a pugilist, but was not nearly agile enough to last ten minutes in the pit with a real fighting dog. There seemed no point in having something that was becoming a mere caricature of its progenitor, that had physical defects without the mental staunchness. After Grip and Rebel, bull terriers bred for dog shows would only have been an anti-climax.

5. Rat Pits and Running Dogs

In my youth, my twin ambition to owning a bull terrier had been to own a whippet. As a child I had lain abed on light summer evenings, and been kept awake by such a shouting and yapping and hollering in the field by my window as might well have awakened the dead. If was Alf Sargent, our local barber, and his pals training their whippets to 'the rag'.

They were a merry, rumbustious crowd, and I used to stand up in bed to watch what they were doing through the window. They usually had a couple of dogs running, either in training spins, to keep fit, or in trials against the stop-watch. It took four or five men to 'handle' these two dogs, to say nothing of a camp following of shrill-voiced lads, who had come to see the fun and to fall in love with running dogs as I did.

The centre-piece of all this activity was the dogs themselves. They were not quite like the modern show whippet, which is a hunched-up, weak-looking creature, tail tucked so tight between its legs that it appears to be trying to ward off the worst effects of chronic colic. Alf's dogs were fine-built all right, but immensely strong as well; chests bigger, in proportion to their size, than greyhounds; snipy-nosed, sharp featured, dogs with eyes more prominent than greyhounds', feet more catlike and thighs more muscular.

Their size varied enormously, according to what work they were wanted for. Only 'rag racing' was legitimate, but 'rabbit racing' had not entirely died out, though it was as strictly forbidden, by law, as dog fighting and cock fighting. But Alf Sargent usually had a good rabbit dog or two as well as his rag dogs.

Training the rag dogs was more spectacular, and easily understood by a child at his bedroom window. A fairly level 'track' was paced out along the footpath across the field, usually 200 yards long. The dogs had arrived muffled up with whippet rugs, muzzled in leather 'box' muzzles, and held on leads by their handlers as carefully as if they were guarding the safety of some important and beautiful film star. The little dogs, which usually weighed from twelve to twenty pounds for rag racing, leaned and pulled on their wide collars, like shire horses with a timber wagon. Neither their warm rugs nor ugly box muzzles could conceal their gay, high-lifting, prancing step, and their tails arched up over their backs with pride instead of cowering between their legs, like the tails of show dogs do. No need for some moron to hold their heads and tails up when the judge came round.

When all was ready, and the course was marked out, muzzles and rugs came off, the handlers gripped their dogs by the nape of the neck and root of the tail, and a 'rag man' for each dog stood waving his 'rag', or towel, in front of its nose, like the second in a boxing ring. Instead of cooling the dog, though, it had the opposite effect: he went wild with excitement.

Since puppyhood he had always had a piece of cloth to play with. Nearly all dogs love the sound of tearing cloth. If they are allowed to tear things up unchecked, they seem to take to it as a natural quarry. Even Alsatians, gripping the sleeve of a fleeing criminal, are trained to chase the rag their trainer waves in front of them, and in the absence of a loose cloth they take naturally to grabbing the sleeve of the hand that should be waving it.

The dog men of my youth would throw a duster in for a litter of pups to worry before they left the dam. By the time they were ten weeks old they would career about the kitchen, chasing the cloth their master waved in front of them and hang on, swinging clear of the ground, like bulldogs, when they caught it.

By the time they were old enough to train to the track, on summer evenings outside my bedroom window they would leave food and friends if anyone waved a towel at them. They barked to get at it, and the longer their handler restrained them, the higher pitched their yapping grew, until it became almost a scream of hysterical excitement. As they 'warmed up', the rag men backed away, still waving, and inciting them to further frenzy by shouting and whistling and cheering them on, as a huntsman sends his hounds to draw a covert.

When they had backed away 200 yards up the track, the whippets were almost beside themselves, and it behove their handlers to keep a firm hold of the skin at the back of their necks or they would writhe round and bite like adders to be freed. When they reached fever pitch the starter would cry, 'Ready, Steady, Now!' and fire his pistol.

On the command 'Ready' the handler would lift all four feet of his charge clear of the ground, at 'Steady' he would swing him back an arm's length, and with the crack of the pistol he would swing his charge forward, loosing it in mid-air at the end of the swing. A good handler could 'throw' his dog five yards up the track to land him smoothly in his stride at full speed. It took a lot of practice with the dog, of course, to acquire his utter confidence, but it was partly this superb team-work 'twixt man and dog that gave the sport its charm.

Within a fraction of a second of the pistol's crack, the dogs were yards away, going at full speed up the track towards the rag, which waved at them like a target. Everybody roared with excitement, the only silent creatures on the track being the whippets, who had stopped their own screams the instant they were slipped and could translate their impotent yells into the action of one mad rush at the rag.

It required great skill to be a clever slipper, but the rag man must be competent at his job too. It was easy enough to incite the dogs at close range with the rag, but he had to have a carrying voice or a piercing whistle to hold their attention at 200 yards range and the best rag men got almost as excited as their dogs. Excitement is a most infectious emotion. The moment he was free to race, the dog was silenced by the concentration of every sinew straining to tear the coveted rag. The rag men continued shouting their encouragement, but icy calm was necessary too. The dogs leaped the last two or three yards to grab the rag in mid-spring. If the rag man stood behind it, his dog would collide with him, full toss, at anything up to forty miles an hour. This would be painful to the man but could be disastrous for the dog, causing him to break a leg or ribs or even neck.

If, on the other hand, the rag was held at the side of the man, firm on rigid arms, the wrench as it snatched the dog from full tilt to a stop, within a foot or so, could be almost as damaging. The correct technique was to hold the rag, at arm's length, to one side and to spin right round at the very instant he grabbed it. The dog would then change direction from a straight line down the course to a full circle as he clung on to the rag and swung round, the rag man being the pivot, to be brought to a gentle standstill as he completed his circle with smooth deceleration.

The manœuvre was less complicated than it sounds, but it did demand split-second timing and superb team-work between man and dog. It was so rapid that I watched it night after night, standing on my bed, before I could piece the exact routine together. I saw young dogs, mere pups, learning to run a few yards for the sensual pleasure of ripping and tearing at the rag for their trouble. I saw them develop a dedication for their task, which bade them ignore the dog they were running against, his handler and friendly strangers, and all the temptations of the world outside their own home. It taught them to think that nothing on earth was as important as getting their teeth into their beautiful, soft towel and ripping it as if it had been their worst enemy.

This training was quite the most important item in a running dog's career. If he was half-hearted about it he would gallop up the course in that wonderful lithe rhythm that only whippets have. He would look very pretty, a poem of motion, but he would be seconds slower over 200 yards than if he were really trying. A dog that was a little mean, on the other hand, that put as much effort into catching and 'killing' his rag as my bull terrier put into catching a rat, would strain every sinew aud muscle so that he would literally be spent in a couple of hundred yards, and, if you tried to make him run farther, would begin to wilt and fade to slower speeds.

Alf Sargent and his pals were artists at getting their charges so keen that they would run themselves to a standstill for the sheer sport of it. They hooted and shouted and laughed and cursed with such enthusiasm that not only did their dogs catch their mood, but I did too. I saw the best side of running dogs, their gay fervour and their affectionate delight in their bosses' praise when they ran well. Sooner or later, I decided, I would have a running dog of my own.

Meanwhile, I was as keen to learn the tricks of the trade as the dogs themselves. I was not allowed to go over to Alf's barber's shop to have my hair cut because his clientele spent most of their time discussing dog racing and horses, bookies and prices, in language which my parents thought I should not hear. So Mohammed came to the mountain. On Sunday morning, about once a month, he came over to our house to cut my father's and my hair by the fire in the waiting-room. I was still too small to sit in the chair and had to kneel on the seat to bring my head to a convenient level. Alf hissed like a groom, continually blowing the loose hair in beery gusts from his scissors. His round cheeks were inflated to the size of a trumpeter's, and when he stopped blowing for a moment, his merriment came out in gales of laughter at the questions I asked about his dogs. He told me that they wore muzzles because he fed them so carefully that he could not risk them picking up a scrap of food he did not know about. They must have been very uncomfortable muzzles too. Box muzzles they were called, though they looked more like horses' nose-bags. Made of cylindrical leather, fairly soft and liberally perforated to allow free breathing, they still prevented the dog from picking up the tiniest morsel of unauthorized food. It always surprised me how little they irked their wearers, who spent so much of their time rugged and muzzled that they seemed to forget their constriction.

Alf told me that the only real way to muscle a dog up was to give him plenty of road work. And he meant work. The purpose of the soft, wide collar that whippets wore was to enable them to lie on it and pull, as bull terriers do, without choking. Most people train their dogs to walk civilly at their side on a slack lead, giving no more trouble than a shadow. Running dogs and fighting dogs were taught to work, to shove with all their might with their back legs so that their weight was taken on their collar and their front legs pawed an inch clear of the ground. Any walking on hard roads tightens feet and brings muscles up like knots. Pulling their whole weight on a hard road made muscles as hard and rip-pling as a professional weight lifter. To encourage them to pull, the bull terrier men used an assistant to walk a few yards ahead with another dog, and the whippet men's assistant simply had to wave a towel occasionally.

But feeding was the secret. You could get your dog's muscles hard with road work and his wind good with train-ing gallops. He still had to be strong to win. I was far too young in Alf Sargent's day to grasp the niceties of feeding, and am only just beginning to understand them now, more than forty years later.

Even in those days, however, I set my heart on a whippet.

The only dogs I had seen tried were Alf's rag dogs, and a great many of the best were only about fourteen pounds in weight. Delicate little dogs, gentle and kind and friends with all the world. As a great treat, he used to bring one with him sometimes, when he came to cut our hair. He would wrinkle his delicate nose at the stink of antiseptics which pervaded the air from the surgery next door, and come to me for fuss and fondling. His skin was fine and his coat silky, and Alf would take his rug and muzzle off, so that he could curl up in front of the gas fire when we were too busy to pay attention to him. His idea, I think, was that I should be allowed a puppy, and I have no doubt, if I had, that I should have become a sort of mascot for the local running dog men. They were such a kindly lot, and they resented the slur of 'ruffians' that clung to them because they fought and wrangled and swore a lot among themselves. If the child of 'respectable' parents had a whippet, they felt it would show that the sport was not as black as it was painted.

I did not get my whippet for years. It was to remain at the head of my unrequited wants—perhaps inflated more than lifesize because of it—until I was able to please myself.

The reason for the small size of so many good whippets was the handicapping system. The dogs were weighed before a race, and the heaviest dog was allotted the back mark, or 'scratch'. His rivals had one yard start for every pound they were lighter. So, if two dogs were running a match, the one weighing twenty pounds and the other fourteen pounds, the smaller dog received six yards start, which slightly favoured it. Whippet racing was one of the few sports where it was not true that 'a good big 'un will beat a good little 'un'.

This handicapping might be still further modified because of the slippers. An exceptional slipper could easily steal a yard from one who was less gifted, and his dogs might be handicapped because of him as well as for their own weight.

The real hall-mark of a slipper was his ability to 'beat the bost'. That is to say his dog had started up the track *before* he heard the report of the pistol. He held it poised by neck and tail, swung it back on the command 'Ready', and forward in a smooth sweep. Instead of listening for the crack of the pistol, the 'bost', as Alf called it, he *watched* for the flash, and his co-ordination was such that he loosed it then, stealing the difference in time between sight and sound. And, perhaps, a bit by anticipation!

Hard muscles and good wind were not enough by themselves. A slipper with reflex reactions as quick as light, and a rag man who was a canine psychologist capable of inciting the selfless enthusiasm of a missionary would help. But the dog still had to be well. 'Well', the Black Country understatement which signified utter perfection of physical fitness.

It is often said that the whippets of those days fed better than the family, better even than the children. This was not as wicked as it sounds in these easy, affluent times. A really good dog, in peak condition, could contribute more to the family exchequer than his master. If he won one important race, he could bring in stakes and side bets far above a week's earnings of his master. If he was not well—and he couldn't be if he was not fed right—he merely wasted whatever time and effort and food were expended on him.

Like fighting dogs, whippets had to carry as much muscle as possible, but no fat. The general principles of diet were just the same. Get the dog 'down' by purging and sweating, until he was below his fighting, or running, weight and did not carry one ounce of superfluous flesh. Then bring him back to weight by a little food of the very highest quality. Alf fed mutton, but he cut every scrap of fat from it before he boiled it. He gave eggs and sherry and calves' foot jelly and minced lean beef. He weighed his dog every day and he weighed the food he gave it, regulating the quantity according to the weight he was trying to gain or lose. Nothing was given for twenty-four hours before a big race except a mouthful of egg and a taste of sherry. The box muzzle was no ornament nor piece of theoretical gear. It made certain that a dog with an

93

appetite made keen by hunger never got one scrap he did not authorize.

Naturally he stood a good chance of winning. He was such a judge of a dog that he could often buy one because of a potential which had not dawned on its owner. He had forgotten more about training than some of his rivals would ever know, and he could outplay plenty of professional dieticians at their own game.

Such knowledge had its handicaps. He was always a force to be reckoned with, and the very fact that a dog was in his name would shorten its odds.

There were various ways of manipulating odds a little, some legitimate and others a bit shady. He might run a dog a few times well below the peak of condition, to try to establish its form and pull a bit of wool over his rivals' eyes by letting them assess it below its true capacity. I don't think he went further than that, but some of his rivals did. One man I know ran a smoke-blue 'bitch' of mediocre ability at a chain of meetings, where 'she' not surprisingly got written off as an outsider. Then he turned up with 'her' for a big race. Nobody took much notice, because his pal's dog was hot favourite. When the race was run his 'bitch' went ahead in the first fifty yards—and stayed there. It was no coincidence that the rag man caught 'her' almost before 'she' was over the line and got 'her' rugged up. Nor was it a coincidence that the rug was obviously cut for a bigger dog.

The 'bitch' which had won was not the same that had been weighed in at the beginning of the meeting, nor was she the 'bitch' which had established long odds the last few times 'she' had run. Indeed, 'she' was no 'bitch' at all, but an outstanding dog with nothing in common but colour. He was a 'ringer', or changeling, his owner had 'rung the changes' with him between weighing in and running the race, and he was changed again with the bitch, who was supposed to have won, within seconds of the race ending. The chief sufferers, of course, were the bookies, and strangers who backed the favourite. There was almost every shade of dodge between plain dishonest, like that, to the more questionable establishments of odds by running unfit, which is still practised on the 'flapping', or unlicensed, greyhound tracks.

Perhaps the person in the best position to influence apparent form was the slipper. He could inch a dog ahead of his rivals by beating the bost fairly or by deliberately slipping just before the gun went off. The flexing of a trigger finger might be easier to work to than the flash of the gun.

A less reputable wrangle was holding a dog *after* the bost, to make him appear worse than he was. A first-rate rag dog would cover 200 yards in twelve seconds, or more than sixteen yards in every second. A lag of a mere tenth of a second after the crack of the pistol would 'slow' the dog almost two yards behind his rivals, and a great many races were won by less than two yards. Occasionally the stewards would have a slipper up before them and accuse him of holding back his dog, but it was a very difficult thing to prove. What would have been deliberate holding in a first-rate man could well have been a good start by one less experienced. A pint of beer before a race could dull a man's reflex more than a tenth of a second, and it was practically impossible to prove he wasn't trying.

The excuses made when stewards did have a show-down could be pretty far-fetched, too. One old rascal I know, who has made his living 'working the trains' with 'find the pea under the thimble', and the 'three card trick' and rigged games of poker, said he was sorry but he didn't hear the bost. He could still hear a policeman's rubber soles above the hubbub of bookies at a racetrack, and another time he said he had got his 'finger stuck in the dog's collar'!

But even sharper practice was concerned with 'bumping'. If an owner entered more than one dog at a meeting, it was the usual procedure to split them up into heats before drawing lots for the dogs they would run against. So a group of friends would all enter their dogs under one name, sometimes agreeing, as well, to share any prize money that accrued. The side effect was that their dogs would be so split up among heats that there would be no chance of them knocking each other out in the preliminary bouts, and with any luck several of them would end up in the final. One dog, perhaps, was up amongst the front markers, and another on scratch, or at any rate near the back. They would weigh up the opposition very carefully, and if, as was probable, the greatest danger came from a rival somewhere near the back mark, they would deliberately sacrifice the chances of one of their own dogs, handicapped near the front, in order to 'nobble' him. The slipper would hold him immediately after the bost and let him go so that his rival was just coming by at that instant. Instead of slipping him in the centre of his own lane, his line would be deviated just enough to make him collide with his victim, who would almost certainly stumble and check, to allow the gang's back marker to go through to win.

When whippet racing died out after the Great War, the breed was nearly lost. Undoubtedly there had been a fair amount of jiggery-pokery in dog racing—there still is—so that it was not considered the thing for a respectable person to own a whippet. Men are judged by the company they keep. So are dogs, and whippets were supposed to belong either to poachers or to gamblers and cheats, as some of them did. But I knew a good many of the real dog men of those days, and their point of view was slightly different. The fun they got from their hobby was not just gambling, not just putting their money on some dog at a greyhound track, which might as well have been a spot on a dice for all they knew of it personally. They loved the gamble and the element of chance, but what fascinated them more was their team-work with their own dogs. They got a thrill from seeing their dogs beat other people's and from knowing that the dog could not have done it without their help in clever feeding and training. The line between black and white tactics on the track, between straight and crooked, was only a hair's breadth.

Holding a dog a few times, or running him not quite fit until the odds were right for a killing, might be sharp practice to outsiders: they regarded it as all in the game.

By the beginning of the Second World War there were very few whippets about, because greyhound racing had about wiped out all but the show dogs. Large numbers of greyhounds are kept and trained on the tracks by professional licensed trainers. They are subject to veterinary inspection before they run, and their previous form is printed on the programme, which states clearly the time taken by the winner of the last race in which they ran, their time for an official trial if they have not raced recently, or gives some other indication of their form. Furthermore, greyhounds are started from boxes, or 'traps', which open mechanically to ensure that all have a simultaneous start. There was more confidence in the integrity of greyhound racing, because any chicanery was, at least, more difficult and less obvious; the money involved was greater, and whippet racing died a natural death.

It revived, in the Midlands, in the latter half of the 1950s. A club was formed with headquarters at The Old Cross Guns, Cradley Heath, where all the dog men who kept fighting dogs used to go. Dog fighting was finished, and the last of the men who really knew how to get a dog well welcomed the return of whippet racing with open arms, and started to teach the younger generation the tricks. Or some of them! The miners of Cannock Chase started clubs at Brownhills and Hednesford, the potters of North Staffordshire joined in, and it is now possible to see whippet racing on a small scale on various colliery sports grounds and local football pitches on Sunday mornings, and larger meetings, almost on the scale of the old days, at Bank Holiday times.

Some clubs insist that dogs shall have 'papers' before they can race. That is to say they must be pedigree whippets, registered at the Kennel Club. Others, particularly up in the Potteries, have so many dogs with 'broken hair' that no one would believe them to be pure whippet, whatever papers they brought. The reason for these 'broken coats', or harsh, wiry hair, instead of the silkiness of pure whippets, was that some of the pedigree dogs were found to be so nesh that they did not really try. They would gallop up the track but would not get down to real racing. So an outcross of Bedlington or terrier was used, the progeny of which was crossed back to whippet. The second generation, which had three-quarters pure whippet blood, would be harder and meaner than his grandsire, but probably betray the fact that his blood was not blue by his harsher coat.

There were still a few old-timers who had kept the racing blood pure simply because they would not have felt right without a real running dog. After a lifetime of scheming how to win races, the problem of getting papers for a dog whose parents were not 'in the book' presented no great difficulty; and so the situation arose where newcomers, with dogs not up to the job, were matching themselves against old-timers who could still lay hands on a few of the right sort.

It nearly finished the revival. If handicapping was on the old lines, where a dog had to concede a yard start for every pound excess weight he carried more than his rivals, good little ones slipped by old hands would win every time, and this would naturally discourage the novices. The broken-haired lurchers of the Potteries, on the other hand, were so very much stronger that it was equally difficult to handicap them fairly.

So instead of handicapping by weight—or by height at shoulder, as the custom used to be in Lancashire—the modern custom is to handicap on form. An unknown dog goes amongst the back markers and is allowed an additional couple of yards start for each race he does not win. The winner of a race goes back a yard for each win, until he ends up on scratch.

If this was carried to absurdity, a pekinese could win in the end! In any case, it is supposed to give everyone the chance of an occasional win, and it must at least be some encouragement to the mugs, who could never compete, on level terms, with skilled dog handlers.

So far as the old hands are concerned, if they are likely to be handicapped if they win, until inferior dogs can beat them, they will either drop out and leave the job to mugs and exhibitors or they will make sure they don't win until the odds are just right. One way they have tried to do this is by 'clever' slipping, and the officials running race-meetings have tried to counteract it, first by preventing them 'throwing' the dog at the start. This demands so much skill that it does give an immense advantage to the good man, as opposed to good dog, and in Alf Sargent's time slippers were handicapped on ability and dogs on form. Now a dog must start with all four feet on the ground, so there is nothing a slipper can do—apart from a sly shove, which may make the dog stumble—to get him up the track quicker. He can still slow him a fraction, if the odds are not right for a win, by 'getting his finger stuck in his collar'! To get over this some clubs have now got a set of boxes, like miniature greyhound traps, and the dogs start from these.

Anyone who has ever been to a whippet race, even a modern one, would not lay big odds on the chances of re-moving scope for individual 'initiative'! It even takes a crowd to weigh them in, and I have seen arguments, verging on fisticuffs, about ounces in the weight of dogs which have just been weighed on cheap little spring balances not accurate to less than half a pound. The dogs run between tapes now, like athletes on a track, in an attempt to prevent bumping of faster dogs coming up behind, and there are a series of pegs to indicate where slippers must stand to give their dogs the right amount of start. But the amount of shuffling up a peg that goes on when the starter is not looking is as amusing as the race itself.

I said that, when I was a child, Alf Sargent had dogs for two kinds of races, rag and rabbit. Rabbit racing was really illegal, because the law forbade the baiting of a captive rabbit with as much vehemence as it forbade dog fighting. The death knell of both was really sounded by the 1911 Cruelty to Animals Act, though both took some time to die.

Most rabbit running was carried on at the back of the pubs frequented by the ironworkers and colliers of the district, the two most famous being The Cross Keys, at Hednesford, and The Robin Hood, at Darlaston. Both had football pitches at the back, and The Cross Keys still has, though it is now mainly used for football. But before the Great War, and just after, they used to have all sorts of fun and games there. Monday afternoon was the great day, because there were still men who, not having spent all last week's 'beer money', did not go to work at all, or, in some cases, had an official half-holiday. 'Saint Monday' they called it in the Midlands.

The Robin Hood at Darlaston was run by a famous family called Wilkes, who were at least as keen on sport as their customers were. On the running ground at the back of the pub they held 'foot races' for customers, ranging from hundred-yard sprints to ten-mile marathons and rag races for dogs. There were even races between dogs and pigeons, because Darlaston was the centre of 'short distance' pigeon racing, which is now as dead as dog fighting. But in those days a strain of pigeon was kept which was ideal for sprint flights. The usual thing was to time one's pigeon home from your rival's loft, and then time his pigeon from your loft to his. Opportunities for manipulation were obvious, so it became a fashion to train a pigeon to fly a short distance—up to 200 yards—not to its loft but to a box held by its owner. There were certain advantages in this, the most obvious of which was that everyone could see exactly what was happening all the time, and the two birds could be raced simultaneously, against each other, instead of separately, against the watch. The advantage that was less obvious was that training a bird not to fly home, but to a box held by its owner on a crowded field, was one of the most difficult forms of training imaginable. A pigeon flyer could take as great legitimate pride in persuading his bird to fly 'to the box' at all, as he could in winning a difficult race. The method he used was to pair the bird he wanted to fly with a hen which was kept in the box, in sight but out of reach, so that he could not mate her. He became so obsessed with his passion that love overcame his homing instinct, and he would fly through a crowd of people with an eagerness which his natural urge to fly home could never impart.

It was natural that pigeon flyers, who had reached such pinnacles of their art, should be eager to demonstrate their skill and to boast amongst their friends in the bar-parlour of the prowess of their birds.

As a result, matches were frequently made between a champion bird and a champion dog, because every fancier felt he had 'the best dog or bird in England', and if his friends and neighbours acknowledged it to be really exceptional, it soon became 'the best in the world'!

The field at the back of The Robin Hood saw dozens of such matches, and the relative speeds of dog and bird were such that the result was usually a sporting gamble either way.

They had sparrow and pigeon shooting contests—live birds, not 'clays'—the occasional challenge, settled with bare fists, between customers; cock fighting on Sunday mornings at the 'Bug Hole', a hollow in the pit banks across the fields; rat pits on Saturdays in the bar; and whippet racing any time.

The least publicized of this dog racing, to avoid attracting the 'undesirable' attention of the police, was running at rabbits. Stronger dogs were used than for rag racing, because a match or a 'ledger' would entail a large number of courses, the climax of each demanding strength for the victor to catch and hold his rabbit.

Two dogs ran at a time, each having a slipper to loose him when the starter fired his pistol. Sometimes they started from the same mark, although it was still possible to give one some start by placing his slipper a measured distance up the courses. In front of the dogs, usually about twenty-five yards away, was a sawdust 'spot' or circle about a foot across, where the rabbit man 'spotted' the rabbit.

Live rabbits were used, usually purchased in bulk from surrounding farmers, who netted them and kept them in lofts or enclosures until they had got enough. Between fifty and a hundred rabbits might be needed for a big meeting.

There was no 'sport' about the game, in the sense that the quarry must always have a fair chance in any true sport. There was nowhere for the rabbit to take refuge, and there are few creatures more stupid than a rabbit 'off his own run.' Flush a rabbit from a 'sit' or form, within striking distance of his own bury, and it takes a very good dog to catch him. He is extremely fast for the first hundred and fifty yards, he weaves round or through or under every bit of cover to baulk his pursuer, and has a wonderful ability for deviating a mere couple of feet from his course, like a rugby three-quarter 'selling the dummy', at the very instant a pursuing dog stoops to pick him up. This slight swerve is almost as effective as the full turn of a hare, and I believe it takes quite as good a dog to catch a rabbit on his own run as a hare, at least until he learns to deal with this deceptive drift in his quarry's course.

A good fox terrier will catch the same rabbit on strange ground. It simply runs, blindly, in too much panic to use any of the cunning adroitness that so often saves its scut at home. It was this unsportsmanlike side to rabbit racing that not only got whippet racing a bad name with the public, but greyhound coursing too. Ignorant fanatics chant an annual malediction on the Waterloo Cup. They say, and newspapers are stupid enough to print what they say, that the greyhounds at Altcar course captive hares. The fact that these critics have obviously never seen the Waterloo Cup, or any coursing meeting, makes no difference to their conviction that greyhound coursing is merely a large brother to the long-illegal whippet racing after bagged rabbits. The fact is that a bagged hare would be as useless for coursing as a bagged rabbit, and it would be equally illegal, so that it would be perfectly easy to stop any coursing meeting using captive quarry and to secure a conviction against those taking part. The Waterloo Cup, and all coursing meetings, merely drive hares across a part of their own territory where it is possible to see what happens when a leash of greyhounds are slipped after them. The hare always has a fair start, it knows exactly where it is trying to take refuge, and the percentage of hares which succeed in making their escape unharmed is probably far higher than in any other field sport, except perhaps falconry.

Rabbit running was an entirely different kettle of fish. An official took a rabbit from his sack, took a grip of it by the loose skin along the back, and held it still for a few seconds on the sawdust 'spot', pointing its head directly away from the dogs and the crowd behind them. When judges and slippers were ready, he loosed the rabbit and gave a shout, to make it run as directly away from the dogs as he could. His shout also had the effect of alerting the dogs. When it got well into its stride and the dogs could both see it, or were 'sighted', the starter fired his pistol and they were on their way. There was no great difficulty or sport in catching the rabbit. It was no better than an animated 'rag', except that it added a further element of chance to the game. However fast a dog or skilful his handler, luck might favour his opponent by persuading the rabbit to veer his way, or favour him by the way it ran. The dog which actually caught the rabbit was the winner. In greyhound coursing it is the dog which contributes most to catching the hare which wins, irrespective of which dog happens to 'lay his mouth on' first.

A match between two dogs might be for the best of, say, twenty-one or more rabbits, so that stamina and guts were almost as important as speed. Or dogs might have a large number of courses in a knock-out competition. For this reason the pure, comparatively delicate little rag dogs, bred for a 200-yard sprint, were hardly strong enough for an afternoon's running at rabbits, and it was common practice to introduce an outcross of various sorts of terrier to toughen the breed. Bedlington, the working dog of the miners up North, was a great favourite. They were fiery little dogs with warm, linty coats, and the more rabbiting or ratting they had, the keener they grew. Another common cross was Irish Terriers, as pugnacious in those days as the natives of their land, bred to tackle anything that moved on four legs, and superb with rats. This cross also produced a dog with more coat than the silky thoroughbred whippet, and more guts and more strength too.

Technically either cross was a lurcher, because a lurcher is any deliberate cross-bred greyhound or whippet, and the ideal aimed at was to get three-quarter whippet blood and a quarter outcross. This could most conveniently be produced by keeping a half-bred stud dog—half whippet and half Bedlington or Irish—and mating him to thoroughbred whippets. The whelps which resulted were almost as fast as the real thing, but a good deal stauncher.

There was another cross that was very popular here in the Midlands. Pit dog—or bull terrier—and whippet, crossed back to whippet. The results were almost indistinguishable from the real thing. The same silky coat and fine whip tail, but a little stronger in the jaw, a little more 'barrel ribbed', perhaps. The thing that gave them away most was that they were more bulbous-eyed. And the odd thing is that, even today, the really good rag dogs that the old-timers produced after the war, from the few dogs they had kept in the family when whippet racing had died out, have still got rather an old-fashioned Stafford Bull Terrier look about them. There is no way of proving it now, as they have Kennel Club registered pedigrees as long as their tails which 'prove' them to be pure-bred. But none of the dog men have much difficulty in getting a set of papers for a pup if they really want to, and my belief is that the winning dogs at the rag today go back to the old-fashioned breed with a bit of devil in it.

This bit of devil was invaluable to a dog running up to

twenty times in an afternoon. Any good rag dog would probably beat him to the first two or three rabbits, but it takes staunch guts to go on trying when fatigue sets in. Furthermore, a dog with the fire of fighting dogs in his veins was often very jealous of his rabbit, and would catch hold of a rival as soon as look at him, when he had killed his quarry. Even on the run-up some of these very 'hard' dogs would growl, and make even a faster dog hang back if he was a bit timid, so that determination could compensate for some deficiency of speed, especially as the match wore on.

With rabbit running there was slightly less scope for the slipper to influence the results than in racing after the rag. It was not so easy to steal a yard at the start if you did not know which way the rabbit might break, and with only two dogs running a match, everyone who had backed the other dog was watching pretty closely to see his rival started fairly.

The one chap who could make all the difference was the man who 'spotted' the rabbit. When two dogs were running a match, a fast sprint dog could beat a slower dog, with more staying power, only until he began to fade. So short courses favoured the fast dog, and long courses helped the tough fellow who was game to go on running all afternoon. Some of the rabbits would be freshly caught and others might have been pining in someone's barn for anything up to a week. An experienced man could tell at a glance by the brightness of their eyes and the sleekness of their coats. So he could pick those that were likely to 'go', and favour the staunch dog or the weaker ones that would be caught by the fastest dog without tiring him. Before liberating it, he held the rabbit by the loose skin on his back, and a judicious squeeze would slow it considerably, too.

It was all part of the fun. Instead of flocking to dog tracks as spectators, or watching strange dogs dash briefly across a television screen, men bred their own dogs and spent countless hours 'getting them well' and instilling in them such keenness that they would run until they fell from exhaustion.

And when they got them 'well and keen', they would lie awake long hours scheming how they could steal a march as well. The race itself was the consummation of weeks of mental and physical effort, instead of merely the excuse for placing a bet, as dog tracks are, with no more personality than the spots on dice.

When racing was over, the customers of The Robin Hood —and other little pubs of the Midlands—would adjourn for a trial of skills in the rat pit. It was a game I never saw, because it had finished long before I was old enough to be allowed on licensed premises, and it was practically exclusive to public houses.

It had almost died out by the end of the Great War, but Hairy Kelly was still supplying a few of the rats he caught to the last of the rat pits in the early 1920s.

The pit, or arena, was usually from six to ten feet across, and was surrounded by smooth, solid-boarded walls about three feet six high. Stories of cornered rats leaping at men's throats are very exaggerated. I have never known a rat bite, except in self-defence to discourage someone from holding it, and I have never seen one leap more than two feet six in the air. Rats are, however, very good at climbing. They cannot scale a smooth vertical wall, but they will run up the corners of most bare brick walls almost as easily as if they were ladders. All that was necessary to prevent their escape from rat pits was a triangular piece of slate or metal, about nine inches across, so fixed as to prevent them climbing out of the corner.

The rat pit in The Robin Hood was in a big room by the bar, and the rules of the competition were by no means complicated. One dog was put into the pit alone with a number of rats, because with two dogs it would have been impossible to decide which had killed most rats, and in any case, the chances are that many of them would have ignored the rats to fight each other, since bull terrier blood ran in the veins of most good rat dogs.

A match might be made between two or more dogs to settle which of them could kill twenty or a hundred rats in the shortest possible time. An alternative was to match dogs to kill as many rats as their weight in pounds in the shortest time. Like dog racing, this favoured little dogs, because a little dog, of about ten pounds' weight, could usually kill ten rats quicker than his bigger rival, of twenty pounds, could kill a score. It was mainly for this sort of competition that the little Yorkshire and Manchester terriers were developed, though it would be interesting to test how long it took a modern show 'Yorkie' to kill eight or ten of Hairy Kelly's specials.

The customers of The Robin Hood preferred the matches where fifty or a hundred rats had to be killed. Black Countrymen adored superlatives. The man who could run a hundred yards quicker than anyone in the world was their idol, and they loved a dog which could kill an impressive number of rats quicker than any other dog, a liking which was very good for Hairy Kelly's trade.

When all was ready for a match, the customers would gather round the pit, their pint pots charged, with jugs to fill them up. The rats were solemnly counted in, one at a time, and note was taken that they all appeared to be fit and sound. They scurried round first, to find any way of escape, or any cover under which they could hide. When they discovered the whole place was as bare as a bald head, they did the next best thing: they huddled in rucks in one corner and the master rats, the biggest and strongest, shoved themselves into the centre of the heap, so that the less wise and the weaker were exposed first to any danger which might threaten.

Danger was not long in coming. Whichever dog was drawn to compete first was carried to the pit by his handler, or setter, and shown the rats. He could be held as near to them as the setter liked, provided his feet did not touch the floor of the pit, so that it was easy enough to be certain he knew where his quarry were. But he might do more harm than good by getting the dog too excited or too close before the match commenced, because either would panic the rats and scatter them in all directions. When the setter was ready he walked round the pit, quietly shepherding odd rats from the corners until they huddled with the rest in one heap. Then he slipped his dog gently into the pit. A novice dog would dash straight into the centre of the rats, undoing his setter's good work by scattering them to the winds, so that he had to chase all over the pit to catch them, wasting valuable seconds as he did so. A clever dog, on the other hand, would slip unobtrusively up to his rats and start killing those at the edge of the pile with one sharp bite and a flick. The whole time he was at it, he would keep a wary eye open for any that tried to sneak away to the other side of the pit, cutting them off the moment they separated from their fellows, and killing them before there was time for them to start a panic. A cool dog like that, which set about his task without uncontrollable enthusiasm, could kill most of the rats in the pit without dispersing them, and he would only have to rip and tear all over the place after the last few cunning survivors who had sat tight and allowed their less intelligent fellows to bear the brunt of the attack for as long as they possibly dared.

When the last rat was killed the setter picked up his dog, the watch was stopped, and the time taken from when his feet first touched the floor of the pit until his setter had gathered him up again. For the time to count, all rats had to be dead, and there was a specific test to decide whether a rat, which might still twitch a little, was officially 'dead' or not. It was put in a chalk circle, about a foot across, and its tail hit with a heavy stick. If it did not move out of the circle, it was counted, but if it did, either the dog had to go back and finish it off, his time mounting up against him, or he was disqualified, or only the number he had killed were counted, depending on the articles of the match.

Having spent a great deal of my spare time ratting, I have never ceased to marvel at the performance of some of these 'professional' rat pit dogs. The best dogs I ever had, or have ever seen, Grip and Rebel, each killed a hundred rats at a sitting. In both cases it was when we were threshing, and catching them was spread over the best part of an afternoon. Both my dogs were bull terriers tipping the scale at between thirty-five and forty pounds, and both were about done-up when they had finished. These pit dogs, though, would have been no good at more than twenty-four pounds, and the majority were about eighteen or twenty pounds. Yet the best of them could kill a hundred rats in less than ten minutes, and the record was about five and a half minutes for the century. As each rat would average three-quarters of a pound in weight and be very capable of hanging on to nose or lips as the penalty for bungling, the physical exertion required constituted no mean feat.

6. The Terrier Man

Bert Gripton was the terrier man to the local hunt when I first met him in 1951. His name was a legend in the area; all hunting folk for miles around knew of him as Gripton, while most other countrymen knew of him as Bert. He was not universally popular, even among the sporting fraternity, because he knew a little too much about foxes. He could, and did, catch them with greater certainty than the hounds, and it was said that he was not above supplying a few to hunts where quarry was scarce. That sort of knowledge is apt to cause professional jealousy amongst the hierarchy of the hunt, and he once got the sack because he was accused of poaching a fox from a neighbouring hunt. It may not have been coincidence that the next eighteen hunting days were blank, and he was eventually reinstated.

He was in favour at the time I met him, and he kept a yard full of working terriers and was paid a small retainer to be available with them, on hunting days; in addition to which, I gathered, he got a small fee for each fox bolted when required. Not a very remunerative occupation, perhaps, but the fact was that he enjoyed foxhunting quite as much as his clients, who were rich enough to go out on horses, and he knew far more about foxes, I believe, than anyone else in the hunting field. He also kept, as a side-line, a few show whippets, one of which hc crossed with a very useful, leggy fox terrier. The pup he kept for himself was a bitch called Tess, very tall for a fox terrier, very strong for a whippet. She was black-and-tan, and about the most unlikely creature it was possible to imagine folding herself up small enough to crawl down a foxhole or artificial drain.

Nevertheless, Tess became as famous as her master, and together they made an unbeatable team. Bert does not look a very big man at first sight, because the depth of his chest, and its breadth, takes from his height. In the immediate post-war years he used to go all over the countryside on an old motorized bicycle, with a wooden platform bolted to the cross-bar with an assortment of grafting spades tied on. Perched, most precariously it seemed, on this platform, were Tess and one or two more conventional fox terriers.

Bert knows as much about the ways of foxes as Hairy Kelly did about rats. Indeed, he knows more, because he can recognize individual foxes, which is more than Hairy ever claimed with rats. Most animals have an extremely well-defined territory and rigid, almost traditional, tracks or pathways for moving about in it. Generations of foxes will use the same gaps in hedges, the same runs along the tops of banks or the sides of ditches, the same earths in woods and same line of country from one wood to the next. They will lie up in fields of kale or corn, wherever they happen to be planted, but when they are disturbed they will seek refuge in the same ancient sanctuaries where generations of their forebears have hidden.

Bert knows all this almost intuitively, and in addition he is exceptionally observant. Not many foxes move in his vicinity without him seeing them, and then he notices where they are heading and he remembers any distinctive marking or colour of their coat or peculiarity in their action. Because they are such creatures of habit, when he sees them again, he always predicts to himself where they will go. He is not always right, of course, but when he comes unstuck, he takes immense pains to find out why and where his judgement went awry, and he adds the permutations of escape-routes or hunting grounds to the store of his memory, so that as years of experience pile up, his margin of error decreases.

It is not as difficult as it might seem to recognize individual animals. All Chinamen look alike to me and all foxhounds look alike to non-hunting folk. Yet other Chinamen and huntsmen can tell their fellows or foxhounds, one from another, with unerring precision. I was reminded of my childhood rabbiting days with Squire Vernon and the collection of foxes' brushes in Hilton Park. I remembered that their colour ranged from fiery red to darkest grey, and I knew that their size varied from a mere ten pounds, no bigger than a good cat, to seventeen or eighteen. So an observant man could undoubtedly store in his mind the images of a large number of individual foxes.

When Bert went hunting he would always try to be ahead of the hounds, always at the far end of the wood they were drawing, the hill on the far side of the valley, wherever he predicted the fox might try to escape. He was careful, as only a non-smoking countryman can be, to stand where wind of him would never blow across the escape-route, never 'head' the fox, or turn him back to be 'chopped' by hounds without a run. He was so used to going among quiet places, where he had not always permission to be, that the bulk of his form merged into dark bushes or trees or hedge, and he could stand as still as an oak stump so that he was practically invisible alike to hunters and hunted. As a result he saw more of the hunt than most. He often saw the fox come several times to the edge of the wood, in different places, before it bolted. Instead of hollering hounds on he kept his own counsel, storing in his mind the 'runs' the fox had thought of slipping through and how much or how little were the strange sounds or sights it had taken to drive him back into the wood again, with hounds to dodge. He noticed which hounds were accurate in their deductions of where he had been and which way he went, and he marked the wastrels, who babbled their noise on the evidence of other hounds' noses. Only when the fox had slipped away did Bert let forth his bellowing holler—and not always then. If he did cheer them on though, hounds rushed with a crash of music, because his was a voice they could rely on, his was judgement they could trust. It was often shrewder than their masters'.

Whether he 'told' the hounds or not, Bert would steal away himself when the fox had gone. His experience told him where it was probably pointing, and he sometimes got there quicker by road than the fox did cross-country. He was not always right, but the line hounds hunted, and the places they eventually either found or lost their fox were valuable clues about what had occurred unpredictably.

In theory, the earth stoppers would have been round the night before, filling the mouths of the foxholes and drains with wood or stones to force the hunted fox to stay above ground. In practice, foxes often lie out like hares in rushes or coarse grass, in rhododendrons and thick bracken, on sunny banks, in long stubble and even hollow trees. Many foxes only use their earths in bad weather and just when they have cubs, so that the job of earth stopping is made more difficult because foxholes are often inconspicuous and apparently disused. On top of this, hunted foxes often go right out of the country where they are found, so that it is impracticable to stop every place they might try.

Sometimes when a fox gets to ground he is left for another day, and sometimes it is decided to dig him out or bolt him, either because he is a skulking devil who has not given a decent run, or because he has been taking poultry or lambs, and the local farmer or landowner either wants him killed or is likely to take the law into his own hands when the hunt has gone. This was when the Master called for Gripton. However far they had run, however remote the place where they checked, he could be relied on to turn up within minutes —if he was not already there! Hounds would be taken to a decent distance while he put his terrier in. Tess, the old half-bred whippet, was one of the best dogs he ever owned. Although she looked so large and reachy, she could crawl down an incredibly small hole, and she had a wonderful knack of persuading Charlie that life would be more certain and healthy outside. In artificial earths, which consisted of a brick chamber, or kennel, with two nine-inch drain-pipes leading from it, she would often lay hold and back out, tugging her fox with her. Bert, who would be waiting, cheering her on in little more than a whisper, would collar her when she got to fresh air again, letting the fox run free for another chance of life. Tess was wonderfully clever at not getting bitten, too. If the fox had his brush towards her that was fine, she caught hold and just lugged him out by brute force. If, as often happened, he had backed up into a 'blind' hole, with only the one entrance, she crouched a few inches away, 'speaking' in a lovely mellow voice, so that her boss could hear where she was, and so that he could dig down to find her with her quarry, if it wouldn't bolt and she couldn't pull it out. But even when the fox presented its 'business end', it is surprising how often she would nail him, nearly always by the nose. It seems that she 'fenced' with him until she could incite him to attack and lunge at her. That was his undoing, for she so balanced herself that she could pin him by the jaws at the end of his stroke, and if he was in a drain, as opposed to a natural earth, she could often pull him out, powerless, with his jaws locked harmlessly shut between her fangs.

If he wouldn't bolt, Bert got busy himself. It was then that his real size and power became apparent, because he seemed to dig with all the power of a human bulldozer, but still with the economy of effort of real craftsmanship. He seemed to know by instinct just when he was getting close to his dog, and then his curved, grafting spade inched the soil gently away, never blocking the hole behind her, in case she had to retreat in a hurry to avoid a direct attack, never so much as catching her the slightest accidental blow.

When he knew exactly where she was, he would sometimes make quite sure that the fox was in a blind hole—at the solid end of his tunnel—before he disturbed Tess. It would have looked a little stupid to have dug down many feet to fox and dog only to have the fox retreat deeper when his adversary was removed. If there was any danger of this, it sometimes paid to dig down at the far end of the fox and make sure by physically blocking his escape.

The function of a good terrier is not to kill foxes, though some of the hard sort will do so only too often. The foot packs of the Lake District are exceptions to the rule and, like their hardbitten Border Terriers, are as lethal below ground as the hounds are above.

Most good terriers are expected to go underground and find their fox, bolt him if he will go, and, if he will not, to stay and face him and 'speak to him'—or bark at him continuously. This is an effective method of holding his attention, because, should he decide to dig further in—which badgers are more likely to do than foxes—the terrier nips in smartly and bites his backside, persuading him to face round the other way in defence, and stay where he is.

It is not all plain sailing, even when sufficient earth has been removed to expose the dog. The first thing to do is to 'tail' her, which means exactly what it says. A terrier should not have its tail docked to a button but left about four inches long, so that it provides a convenient handle by which he can be pulled backwards from his hole. Gripton would lift Tess clear and pass her to someone to hold, and then gently break away enough tunnel wall to see which way round the fox was facing. If it had turned down the hole he would tail that too by the brush, and drag it out, to let it go when all the rest of the holes were stopped, so that it was forced to give a run for its money and there was no danger of it slipping into another hole. It is anything but wise to hold a fox up by its brush, because it can writhe and twist and has a bite that nobody who has experienced it wants to try again. It is possible, however, to swing fairly slowly round until there is just enough centrifugal force applied to prevent it reaching up. Quite often it was the fox's grinning mask which came into view, in which case there is an effective trick that requires supreme confidence and dexterity approaching sleight of hand. Hold a bit of stick, as thick as your thumb, and about a foot long, and wave it rapidly across the fox's mask, within reach of his jaws. The reaction is reflex and certain. He bites the stick in a vice-like grip. That is the exact split second when it is safe to shoot out the other hand to grab him by the scruff of the neck. It takes more cool nerve than I possess, but it was one of Bert Gripton's star performances.

Tess was by no means his only terrier. He had, and still has, a pack of anything up to a score, all entered to fox and most to badger. One of his favourite pastimes is to join one of the adjacent packs on a day's hunting, and wait until they get into difficulty because their fox holes-up in a drain or in some other difficult spot. When the local terrier man is forced to give it best, Bert, with a deceptively innocent grin, asks if he can help, as he 'happens' to have a terrier with him. The answer is usually 'Yes', and since he is quite exceptional with a spade, and never takes a dog out in public until it really is useful, he often succeeds where others have failed. The onlookers are naturally impressed, and there is sometimes an offer to buy the terrier. 'Couldn't sell him,' is the reply, 'he's the best dog in England; but you can have a pup.' An untried, untrained pup is not at all what is wanted, and often enough the pressure increases until the 'best dog in England' changes hands—at a highly satisfactory figure. But there is usually another 'best in England' out the next week.

I am not particularly fond of hunt terriers. They seem such proper 'little men' to me, all bombast and aggression, all guts and no brains. But I did fall in love with Tess, because she had such an obviously exceptional degree of intelligence to match her courage. An example of this was the mutual attachment she and Lord Wrottesley formed for each other. He was an old man then, but he used to go out in the car whenever hounds were in his area. Promptly at one o'clock, the car was stopped for him to eat a simple sandwich lunch. And whatever she might be doing at five minutes to one, apart from active engagement with a fox, she managed to join his lordship for a share of his sandwiches precisely on the stroke of the hour.

She was just as good with badgers as with foxes. A friend of mine, hearing that 'Gripton would handle a fox with his bare hands', was anxious to see exactly how it was done, so on the spur of the moment we went over to see if he would oblige.

'Certainly,' he said, 'if you'll take me about four miles.'

We piled into the car, complete with Tess, and Bert asked me to stop on a main road. Leaving the car, we set off to walk a few hundred yards up the road, before climbing through a hedge to cross some fields. I was just wondering why we had not parked the car opposite the point we left the road when there was an urgent request to 'keep your heads down, I don't want the farmer to see us'. I had poached some funny things in my time, but never a fox at one o'clock midday. However the hedges were pleasantly thick, and when we had crossed a couple of fields, we came to an artificial earth in a dingle.

The dingle itself appeared to have been dug out by hand at some time in the past, probably for marl to spread on the land. Like most old marlpits it had steep sides, overgrown with selfset hawthorn and blackberry and elder. At each end, twenty-five or thirty yards apart, there was a round hole, nine inches in diameter. These two holes were the entrances to the artificial earth or drain, and unglazed, earthenware pipes joined each entrance to a brickbuilt underground kennel, about the size of an inspection pit in an ordinary household drainage system. The whole thing had been most carefully built, the entrances being a couple of feet or so below the kennel, so that any moisture seeping in was always drained away to leave a beautiful dry foundation for any bedding. The kennel itself was covered by a foot or two of earth, so that it was completely hidden, and was cool in summer and warm in winter. No doubt generations of foxes had sneaked to it and away on their hunting expeditions, unseen and unsuspected, as we had. Bert said it was a 'sure find' and that if he bolted a fox from it hunting on Saturday he would be back there snug and safe by about Tuesday. Indeed, it had held for years a famous fox that, to his knowledge, had been hunted eleven times and got safely back, only to meet an undignified end by shooting at the finish of a long career. We hoped that one of his sons would be at home today.

Before doing anything at all, Bert took a wire from his pocket, fashioned from the inner brake cable of a bicycle, with far more 'spring' than a normal snare. One end had been soldered round a metal eye, originally fitted to the lace-hole of a pair of army boots, and the other end was fastened to a tough cord. The eye made a noose that not only closed sweetly, to imprison any neck that was thrust through it, but that opened smoothly as well, so that the captive could be released without damage. This was where the springy wire assisted. He tied the cord to a fairly heavy fencing post, which would 'give' and drag a little, rather than slam the noose to with a jab, as a solid anchorage would do, set the noose at one of the drain-pipes, and left me to watch it and tell him quietly when Charlie bolted.

'Quietly,' he emphasized, 'the farmer mustn't hear us.'

Then he took the visitor to the other entrance and slipped Tess in. It seemed most unreasonable to put such a tall and bulky dog in a nine-inch drain pipe. She seemed to fill it, so that she would have no room to manoeuvre and back out of trouble if she was attacked, but she folded herself up into a crouching bundle of muscle and fangs, and disappeared.

A minute went by and nothing came out. Two minutes, then five, which seemed like an hour. The edge of our excitement wore thin and I began to think how stupid we should look if we were discovered. The truth would sound so far-fetched that no one would believe us. 'We were just looking for a fox', would sound as unlikely, out of the hunting season, with the nearest pack of hounds safe in kennels twelve miles away, as the time-honoured 'Just trying to shoot a pigeon' seems in the middle of a pheasant covert.

I wondered if Tess had got stuck at some unexpected bend of the pipe, or if she had found a nest of rabbits and was quietly making a meal of them. Then, deep in the earth, I heard her voice.

'She's speaking, Bert,' I said. 'Do you think he won't bolt?' He came to my pipe and laid his ear to the entrance.

'Hell,' he said, 'that's not a fox. It's a badger—and he won't bolt.'

All dogs have a language of their own, and it is easy to tell, when you know them well, what quarry they are working. Tess had a much harder, more insistent bark, when she was speaking to badger than if she was only sharing the pipe with a fox. It was an urgent, almost hysterical note, because she knew her slightest error could be costly. Foxes make slashing, painful wounds, liable to go septic afterwards, but they cannot crush as a badger can. He has about the strongest jaws in the world, for his size.

There was only one thing to be done, and that was to open up the kennel and see exactly where they were. Out at the far side of the dingle we emerged into an open, sloping, turf field. It sloped gently down to a farmhouse about two hundred yards away. The front of the house stared up at us, and a brilliant sun shone down like a spot-light on the stage. We could only hope the farmer was having his lunch in the kitchen. If he had been in the dining-room he could not have failed to see us. Bert pulled a shortened but business-like little grafting spade from his immense poacher's pocket, and clods of earth started to fly as if a silent bomb had dropped. He really was in a hurry, moving more earth at a stroke than any two other men I ever saw. In a few moments he had come down to the timber lid of the kennel, made of solid railway sleepers; and seconds later it was off. All that we could see was the bricked chamber of the kennel, about three feet by two and eighteen inches or two feet deep. The two pipes entered at each end of one side, providing some ventilation without too much draught; and the floor of the kennel was deep in warm bracken, dragged in by the house-proud Brock. Tess was silent by now, but we knew she must be in one of the two pipes leading out of the kennel, and Bert shoved his head down to hear which one.

'Good bitch,' he said, 'get to him, get to him.'

There was much grunting and scuffling, and steamy breath rose from one pipe in a faint haze. Then the rear end of Tess came into view, struggling and tugging until her back feet came out of the smooth pipe on to the rougher floor of the kennel, where she could really take the strain. Without a moment's hesitation Bert pushed a hand over her back and neck, and lay groping for something he could not see in a pipe where he knew war was being waged between his bitch and a badger. It seemed utter madness, and I was certain that, when he took stock of his fingers, he was bound to find some missing. He tensed, and I saw his back muscles flex. Then he shoved his other hand down, caught hold of his dog and handed her up to me.

'Don't loose her,' he said, 'whatever you do, hang on to her.' If I had loosed her she would have been back in the hole in a trice, and might well have laid hold of her master's hand by mistake. Bert lay there, pulling and tugging. He half rolled over, so that he could get on to his knees, still tugging at something down the hole; and we couldn't believe, if it was a badger, that Tess could have killed it so quickly.

I have met lots of people, particularly bull terrier men, who claim to own a dog that will kill a badger. They may own a dog that can kill a cub or some wretched creature that has fretted until it has almost died in captivity. But I simply do not believe anyone who says he has a dog which can kill an adult, healthy, wild badger single-handed, and I have more than once seen badgers escape from a pack of foxhounds, not because they could run fast but simply because they were too tough, they could bite too hard, and they were gamer than the hounds. Knowing this, I was certain that Tess, a half-bred whippet, could not have killed the badger in our dingle, and it seemed the very height of folly for her master to be crouching there, tugging away at something he could not see. Seconds later he triumphed. Slowly he dragged a great boar badger out of the pipe and into the kennel by its tail. With a triumphant grin he swung it clear of the ground, and slipped it into a sack with the dexterity of a juggler.

At the time we thought it about the most foolhardy trick we had ever seen. Very few men will tail a badger with their bare hands when they can clearly see exactly what they are doing. To stuff one's hands up a pipe where a badger was being tackled by a terrier appeared to be asking for trouble in the most certain way. I had known him for a long time though, and had never had any cause to doubt his sanity before. When I analysed the sequence we had just watched, I realized he had not departed from a sensible course this time either.

We had first heard Tess speaking to the badger deep in the drain. It was a fair assumption that she had come up to him, when he was lying in the kennel, and that he had faced up to her and barred her progress. Like the good working terrier she was, she had just kept out of his reach and given tongue with enthusiasm to let us know what was happening. She probably went on speaking while her master was digging down to the roof of the kennel, and as she heard help getting closer, she would get bolder and more excited. So long as Brock stayed in the kennel there was a chance she would squeeze in too and join battle. Besides this, he would sense his danger growing as help dug nearer down to them. Eventually he would decide to retreat to the constriction of the nine-inch drain, and as he turned, Tess would take hold of a good mouthful of badger ham.

On reflection it was obvious that the old bitch would still have been speaking if the badger's business end was facing the kennel, which it would have been if he had backed down the pipe. The very fact that Tess had found it possible to go in and lay hold implied that she had caught a grip of somewhere fairly safe. Bert had slid his hand along the top of her head, to feel what it was she was holding, and when he found the badger's tail he had calculated it was safe to get his dog off and bring Brock out himself.

I became a great admirer of Tess, not just for her prowess below ground, but because of her wisdom as well. At night, for example, if anyone was about, she would come bustling into the back of her master's legs. Even if you are neither trespassing nor doing any harm, it is still a comfort to know that there is a stranger or a keeper about before he has time to realize that you are there. She was a wonderful dog with rabbits, too. The half whippet blood in her veins made her fleet enough to catch one fair, in her prime, but she could still pounce on one in a 'sit', when she was an old dog. The terrier in her make-up gave her a good nose, so that she could hunt a line as well. She was obedient and affectionate, an ideal dog to have for a country companion.

Nobody as fond of sport as Gripton could resist the temptation to try his whippets out as well as to show them. They were not very successful, because, running rabbits on rough ground, it was never very long before they broke a leg. Having such fine bones and delicate little legs made it especially difficult to set them well, so that there were usually one or two obvious accident cases about. A whippet club has been formed this last two or three years, with the specific object of coursing hares. They are very fast over a short distance, and come to no great harm in open, level country. But used anywhere that rabbits frequented, as Bert's were, there would soon be some cripples about.

When one very good dog broke a front leg, it was decided to mate him to Tess when he recovered, to try to give his progeny a little more stamina and a little more toughness. The pups would be whippet lurchers, three-quarter whippet and one-quarter terrier from Tess. I remembered the whippets of my childhood, the working rabbiting dogs of Alf Sargent, and my ambition to own a whippet flared up again. Nothing would do for me until Bert had promised me a pup.

Dinah cost me thirty shillings. She was a fawn-smut, less black and more tan than Tess, but very like her, especially about the face. She is thirteen now, subject to little heart attacks and over-fond of her food; and she spends long hours on the drawing-room sofa. But her eyes and ears and teeth are as good as a young dog, she is still game to try for rats or mice, and is very offended when I stop her, in deference to her age.

Oddly enough she was a particularly late starter. As a pup she was very sensitive, shy and easily offended, and she nearly died from fits, brought on by some new-fangled worm medicine of the time, which was supposed to dissolve them. Most terrier pups will kill rats when they are six months old, but at nine months she was so gentle she would not harm a rabbit. I had long since broken her to ferrets, so I put a bagged rabbit in a hen-run and introduced her to it. Shades of Alf Sargent and his rabbiting dogs! It was exactly what the police would have run him in for—if they had caught him. Dinah played with her rabbit for a while and then she retrieved it for me as gently as a Field Trial Champion. But after that there was no stopping her.

She was a very small bitch for rabbiting too. At twelve months old she scaled eighteen pounds when fit; and bearing in mind the fact that she carried a quarter of terrier blood with sturdy bone, she was never anything like as long in the leg as the old rabbiting dogs were. She had bags of drive though. She was muscled like a ballet dancer, all backside and thighs, with her ribs showing clearly. She had the rather bulbous eyes of the traditional rabbit dogs—with 'a bit of bull in them'—her ears were a trifle large, like Tess's, and her little cat-like feet were neat with white socks.

Even as a youngster she was a good house-dog, with a hard, high-pitched bark, the sort of voice her mother affected when she was close up to her badger. Not that I entered her either to fox or badger, though I did not doubt her ability when once she discovered what fun it could be. She was so gentle and affectionate that I could never stand the idea of getting her cut up by some great badger twice her weight or fox with jaws that made every wound go wrong. Indeed, I have been far too fond of badgers to like digging them out, and for ten years of her life Dinah would allow my own tame badger to play with her and share the hearth-rug on winter evenings. He was a boisterous chap, and when he got too rough, instead of being annoyed with him she jumped on a cushion out of the way, so that no one had the heart to turn her off; she is so graceful and attractive she seems to have been born to a life of gracious living.

I always like my dogs to possess more than good looks though, so I was particularly pleased when Dinah took to that first rabbit. My bull terriers had both died as a result of killing too many rats, so I had decided that a dog to catch 'long-eared 'uns', instead of quarry with long tails, would be just as much fun for me and conducive to a longer life for my dog. And so it has turned out.

My addiction to ratting on Sunday mornings had been the introduction to a host of farming friends. When I turned up with the ferrets, as usual, but a long dog instead of a ratting terrier, they seemed quite as happy to allow me to make free with their rabbits as with their rats.

I used to visit one farm very often, because it was ideal for the job. It had large fields, with hedges on banks which had been thrown up high to make deep ditches, because part was low-lying and needed draining exceptionally well. At one side of the farm was a forty-acre wood, in those days full to overflowing with rabbits; and the land sloped down to a stream flanked by rushy meadows. The farmer was a tenant and the shooting was let. But rabbits are always a loophole. Whatever agreement is made by the owner about sporting rights, whoever rents the shooting, nobody can prevent the farmer, even if he is only the tenant, from catching 'ground game'. That is rabbits and hares. It is a perfectly logical law, because rabbits and hares can do almost incalculable damage to crops, and until the law was amended the farmer had to suffer for the sporting owner's, or tenant's, sport. Now the farmer and his family and one outsider, who must be *employed* to kill rabbits and hares, cannot be prevented by anyone from killing ground game. So I became 'official' rabbit catcher, and though the keeper did not like it he couldn't stop me.

Some of the warrens, or 'buries', were quite small and easily ferreted, but there were a couple of big ones under great trees, where digging would have been practically impossible because of the roots. I used to stink these holes out, at fortnightly intervals, about three times at the beginning of the season. Special liquid is produced, under various trade names, to make holes untenable for rabbits. It smells rather like particularly potent creosote, and I used to soak bits of newspaper in it and put them wet into the holes. They were perfectly obvious to any observant keeper, and although there was nothing he could do about it, I have never believed in trailing my coat unnecessarily. I found that a less conspicuous alternative was to soak sawdust with the liquid and use a long-handled cooking spoon to put a little down all main holes, far enough to keep them fairly dry. Another advantage of this method was that it was much easier to apply without becoming personally contaminated. The stench was so powerful and so persistent if a few drops got on one's skin or clothes that friends turned the other way for days. The result of two or three applications to difficult buries was that the colony of rabbits would often leave them entirely for the season. They congregated instead in the smaller holes, which were easier to ferret, or lay out in forms in the rushy tussocks.

When I went ferreting, my host usually came too and brought his gun. It was a mixed blessing. He was powerfully built and used to hard manual work, so I worked the ferrets and he dug, if they got fast on a rabbit. The snag was that he was rather enthusiastic with his gun. I had the greatest respect for his marksmanship and I never saw him do any damage. But I once saw him and his brother fire simultaneously at the same rabbit—which was almost directly between them. And, far worse from my viewpoint, he once shot a rabbit, which Dinah was coursing, about four feet in front of her nose. My comments were so vivid that we parted extremely abruptly and I never returned for two years.

Ferreting was much more fun with Dinah than it had been with Mick in the old days. I used purse nets then, simply because Mick was not fast enough to catch a rabbit in the open. With Dinah I sneaked upwind to the hole, popped a ferret in and waited. The merest movement would convey to her which way to move or where to stand. It was like the conductor of an orchestra painting the effects he wanted with his baton, except that if I, as conductor, were wrong, my musician would tell me so in no uncertain terms. Normally she would move wherever I signalled, and I put her where I thought the rabbits were most likely to bolt. She would crouch there, quivering with excitement, her great ears straining to catch the first subterranean rumblings, so that she could beat the bost when the rabbit decided to try his luck and bolt. My friends found it impressive to watch me waving her to come nearer or go further away, to shift to right or left, and, without a word being spoken, to watch her immediate compliance.

Sometimes she did not seem quite so quick on the uptake, not quite so easy to put where I thought she would have the best chance. We were so perfectly in tune that I did not press her then. I knew she would not demur without good reason, and our roles were reversed. *I* watched *her* for clues, and would see the slight twitching of her delicate nose, and how her ears, cocked like direction-finders, pointed to where she believed the rabbits and ferret were playing their grim game of hide-and-seek below ground. If we were by ourselves, I just hissed to her 'Get to it', and she would obey her own impulse, based on the evidence of her perceptive senses. If friends were there—and I was playing to the gallery a bit— I would merely sign her to go where I could see she wanted. Although I was preaching to the converted and giving only the orders she wanted, my friends thought I had some sixth sense which told me where rabbits were as unerringly as Dinah's more sensitive ears and nose.

She was a quiet little dog, and she would creep gingerly up to the hole nearest her quarry with such stealth that she hardly ever scared it into staying below ground and taking its chance with the ferret. Nevertheless she stood more chance behind or at the side of the hole, so that the rabbit got clear away from the bury, with no chance of slipping into the safety of another hole before she started in pursuit. So when I had seen exactly where she thought it was, I usually signalled her to stand back two or three yards, and her intelligence was such that she soon understood that giving the rabbit more start than seemed necessary did, in fact, give her a better chance than if she crowded the mouths of the holes.

When our efforts were crowned with success, and a rabbit got clean away, all the trouble was worthwhile. Dinah streaked off in pursuit across the turf, her back arching and straightening with the power of an English long-bow. In whippet racing it is easy to become so enthralled by watching which dog is stealing a head's lead that one misses the sheer poetry of watching a dog run. Dinah and her quarry were alone in the great expanse of turf, and it was obvious how perfectly she had been made for her job, what an ideal running machine she really was, with her immensely deep chest, for her size, and enough heartroom to allow her to outstay pure-bred whippets and to go on running long after they had tailed away in the distance; and legs strong enough to last her ten active seasons over rough ground without damage, but economical, withal, in their bone, so that she didn't carry a spare ounce. The muscles of shoulders and thighs sadly degenerated to fat in her retirement, rippled and flexed and knotted with each enormous, bounding stride. For several seasons she averaged between two and three hundred rabbits caught, and even then she only caught, perhaps, one in every three or four courses. Nevertheless, I have never seen her run without experiencing that feeling of physical excitement in the pit of my stomach, that instantaneous surge of blood as my heart speeds up with her stride, which I only expect on important or frightening occasions.

It was always fun to watch her in competition, because of the thrill when she did well against other dogs. One especially memorable day was when Bert Gripton and I were invited for a day's rabbiting on the Long Mynd at Church Stretton. There were literally thousands of rabbits there before they were smitten by myxomatosis. Our host owned the rabbiting along the sides and top of the hill, and employed a professional warrener, who caught several thousand rabbits a year. He wired some, trapped some, netted some and ferreted some. It is obvious that he could not spend too much time digging odd rabbits out, nor did he want to spoil his easy buries by filling more holes than he could help with his spade. So he used a 'radio ferret'. This was a most ingenious contraption costing about £16, which would have been uneconomic except for use where the potential harvest of rabbits would warrant the expenditure. It consisted of a tiny harness, like old ladies use to take their pet dogs for a walk, but small enough to fit a ferret instead of his collar. A tiny electric coil was fixed to the harness, between the ferret's shoulders, joining the neck collar to the band which spanned the chest. Instead of a conventional ferret line of cord, a flexible, insulated wire connected the coil on the ferret's shoulder to a little transmitter. When a rabbit 'lay up', and the loose ferret stayed with it, a 'liner' was put down to locate it in the normal way. When he found the rabbit and settled down to kill it, the little transmitter was switched on, the current passed down his 'line' and a signal was given off by the coil on his shoulder. This signal was clearly picked up by a small receiving-set connected to ordinary radio earphones, and the strength of the signal—a horrible yowling note like an old-fashioned wireless set oscillating—was inversely proportional to the distance between the coil on the ferret and the receiver; the nearer the ferret, the louder the noise. All the operator had to do was to move around above ground until he received the most powerful note. His line ferret was then directly beneath him, and it was only necessary to dig vertically down instead of trenching several times to follow the line. Dinah was a wonderful bitch to mark a rabbit lying-up, and so was Mick. But Bert and I were vastly intrigued by the mechanical accuracy of this radio ferret.

We were enthusiastic about the sport we had, too. Our host had brought two greyhound lurchers, about twice as big as our little whippets, and we took one side each of the open buries round the edge of the hillside. His dogs were used to the game and would slink about twenty-five yards away from the bury, lie down, ears cocked and muscles all tensed up, waiting for the rabbits to bolt. The fact that they lay so far away from the holes ensured that the rabbits had got quite clear of the buries before they saw their pursuers, and they hardly ever lost one because it got back into the bury it had bolted from. This was very important, because it is almost impossible to make the same rabbit bolt twice. It prefers to bunch itself up in the end of a blind hole, filling the tunnel with its haunches, and waiting for the ferret to do its worst. When the ferret does arrive, no vital part of the rabbit's anatomy is exposed to it, and the ferret will often scratch and bite at the rabbit's haunches for a very long time before either giving up, to go in search of something easier, or getting past and over its back to inflict more effective damage at his head or neck. In either case it means a wait and a dig, though the delay with the radio ferret was far less than it would normally have been.

The type of rabbiting our whippets had done was less open and more in hedgerows, where the rabbit was more likely to beat the dog by diving into the cover of the hedge bottom than popping into the holes it had just left. We had trained our whippets to lie much nearer the holes, near enough to hear which hole the rabbit would bolt from and close into the hedgeside, so that he had to run out into the open to avoid being snapped up in his first few paces. Our dogs were not too popular on this open hillside for a bit, until Bert and I took one each and crouched with it far enough in the open to let the rabbits get clear before starting to chase them. After a few goes, it was surprising how quickly they grasped what was needed. Then they stood yards instead of feet away, and we had the best rabbiting I ever had in my life. In average rabbit country it was a good day to get a score by ferreting. This day, with no nets or guns, nothing but the dogs to catch them, we caught over twenty-five. And although the greyhound lurchers were so much bigger, the distances were short enough to allow our dogs to acquit themselves with honour.

However brisk the fun with ferrets, there is nothing more sporting than walking up rabbits which are sitting out. If they are not disturbed, rabbits will often sit in forms, as hares do, in preference to being crowded in underground holes. By making the holes even less attractive with my stinking sawdust, I was simply making a life in the open air even more attractive. With a practised eye it is quite easy to spot these rabbits sitting out in tussocks or tussocky grass, and they will not move until they are certain they have been discovered. Indeed most country boys, in my day, were very expert at 'picking a rabbit out of a sit'. The trick was to walk steadily on a line which would pass about fifteen inches to the side of the rabbit. If you went much closer than that he sometimes bolted, because he thought your course would lead you directly to step on him. So long as he believed he was undiscovered he would sit tight, so that it was possible to grab him with one deft stoop as you got level, without ever checking at all—or you could put your foot on him if you were too stiff to stoop, and not too squeamish.

But we were not interested in picking up rabbits. It was the sport we went for. The advantage to us of spotting them before they left their sit was that it was then possible to get between them and the nearest cover, call the dogs up, flush the rabbit towards the open field and only slip the dogs when he had got a good start. Then we would watch the whole course and assess which dog was fastest and cleverest, qualities that by no means always went hand in hand. We could revel in the sinuous rhythm as they really got down to business, rejoice with pride if it was our dog which triumphed, and look forward to the next time if, as often happened, the rabbit got away.

It was here that I first discovered that a running dog's worst enemy is barbed wire. The man who invented it should lie on a mattress of it till eternity.

Dinah had coursed her rabbit across a field, and was within a couple of feet of him and gaining fast when they reached the hedge. He slipped clean through the centre of a run, full toss, without checking speed the tiniest bit; and she dived after him. It was the dead of winter, with no leaves to mask what happened, and I saw her somersault the other side of the ditch, give one yelp and carry on as if it was an acrobatic trick she had performed on purpose. She went on and caught her rabbit in the next field, and then came limping back with it. When I got up to her, there was a great raw patch on her thigh that seemed as big as the palm of my hand. She had 'wired' herself going through the hedge, and the barb had jagged a triangular piece of skin which had gaped apart, leaving a wound it took fourteen stitches to mend. Since then my dogs have got repeatedly lacerated on barbed wire, and every time they do, I damn the man who invented it with curses that ought to shrivel his memory.

As she became more experienced Dinah began to find her rabbits for herself. I helped her at first, because when I spotted a rabbit in a 'sit' I did not flush it for her, but called her up and motioned her, with sweeps of my arm and vocal encouragement, to work the ground in that direction. At first she would flush the rabbit—found with my aid—by accident, almost stumbling on it. Then she gained confidence in my signals, and was not only anxious to go in the direction I indicated, but was acutely aware that her quarry was almost certainly ahead.

It was exciting to watch her knowledge swell. The quarter terrier in her blood had endowed her with a good nose, and she tested every eddy of breeze for clues of her quarry. Then, as time went on, she remembered every bush and tussock where she had found one before, and never passed without testing if another was in residence. It was only a step from that for her to learn what sort of places were likely and where it was a waste of time to try. She learnt to quarter the ground like a setter, going as far either side of me as I signalled, and to work a hedge with the thoroughness of a spaniel, so that every walk with her became filled with sporting potential.

At about this time a farming friend of mine bought a government surplus jeep, and we started to amuse ourselves going round his farm with it at night. Nobody who ever went round Harold's farm with him in his jeep in daylight was likely to forget it. It made a cowboy's bucking bronco seem as harmless as a rocking-horse. In the headlights at night, the valleys and humps of ground came up to meet us with nightmare speed, and the ride to the running ground was an adventure in itself.

People who have tried shooting rabbits in headlights at night might not believe coursing them with whippets could be any more fun. Certainly there is no sport in shooting them, for they usually squat, or certainly do not move very fast, because the light dazzles them and they cannot believe there is danger because they cannot see it.

When we went out the technique was to weave gently left and right, so that the beam of the headlights picked out any rabbits grazing a hundred yards or so away. This was not as simple as it sounds, partly because of Harold's enthusiasm and partly because he is a bit left-handed. His enthusiasm incited him to rock the jeep from one side to another so fast that any rabbits ahead only stayed in the beam for the fraction of a second. I would roar 'Steady! Right a bit!' but his exuberance knew no such speed as steady, and his left hand mastery often swung us the wrong way, so that the rabbit was swallowed by gloom again.

The vital thing in this sort of rabbiting was to spot the rabbit as far away as possible and get within about fifty yards, before slowing up to a walking pace and slipping Dinah. By day, fifty yards start would be too much, if the rabbit saw the danger, but at night it did not appreciate the danger until it actually saw Dinah approach. Then, when she was within about ten yards, it set off for home with as much determination as if it was broad daylight. That was the difference between coursing and shooting at night. The quarry gave no sport whatever with a gun, and it would be no more effective to net them and screw their necks. With a dog it was perhaps more difficult and sporting than walking them up, even out of 'sits' in sunlight.

Part of the difficulty was keeping the rabbit in the headlight beam. Running directly away was simple enough, but when dog and rabbit suddenly streaked off to right or left it was often difficult to turn the jeep round fast enough to hold them, and it was by no means unknown for us to topple over. We used to try to let the rabbit get as far away as possible, because then we did not have to swerve and jink so rapidly to keep it in the beam. On the other hand, if we did not get to within about fifty yards before Dinah was slipped, the run-in took too much steam out of her, and she would be blown after a couple of runs. The other snag in being too near was the danger that the rabbit would not appreciate what the jeep was, and would run towards it instead of away. This was by far the worst risk of all, because it would have been all too easy for rabbit and dog to run clean under the chassis and for us to be unable to avoid hitting them. We had several very narrow squeaks like this before we realized the danger, and we had to shout and thump the bonnet and roar like maniacs to turn the oncoming rabbit and make it take a less dangerous course.

This is not so bad on one's own ground. The snag was that it was sometimes possible to go round every field on the home farm and see nothing more interesting than a few roosting larks and meadow pipits flutter up in the headlights. Then Harold's exuberance took charge and we would try his neighbours, who knew us well enough not to mind, or at least to *say* they did not mind. In any case they did not often know, because at that time of night they were usually either getting square eyes watching television, or were safely tucked in bed. But if there were no rabbits out feeding on home pastures, the chances were that a hunting fox, or whatever had dissuaded them from risking their scuts above ground, had had the same effect on those on adjoining land. In that case we went further afield. There is nothing I know of which can make one feel so naked and exposed as charging round the countryside at night, without permission, with headlights ablaze. It seems quite impossible that there can be anyone for miles around who cannot see the lights, the jeep, and who is in it.

The hazard is not quite so enormous as it appears. For one thing there is no noise to attract attention, and there are lots of legitimate lights on roads around; so one which weaves unusual patterns is not necessarily noticed, and catching a quarry with a dog is at least quieter than using a gun. Another thing that helped us was that we never 'worked' more than one field in a district. We opened the gate, slipped round as quickly as we could—loosing the dog and having our sport, if there was one out in the open—picked her up and were off so quickly that nobody seeing us would have had time to do anything about it unless he had the luck to be within a few yards of the gate when we went in.

There were unexpected risks as well. One night we turned into a very big field of stubble and spotted a rabbit on the far side. Harold set course at full speed and I sat by him with Dinah poised under my arm, ready to slip her as soon as he got near enough and slowed down. We never got so near. At one time the large field we were in had apparently been two, divided by a hedge. The owner had grubbed the hedge up but had been inconsiderate enough to leave the ditch. Neither of us saw it until it was too late, and we hit it full toss. Harold was holding the steering-wheel, which prevented him being thrown forward. I was holding Dinah, and continued at undiminished velocity until I was stopped by my head hitting the windscreen support. I remembered nothing more for several seconds, and when I did come round I found myself lying on the stubble looking up at the lights. My instinct for self-preservation is fairly well-developed, and I suggested to Harold, very clearly and forcibly, that he turn the lights out before the whole of the local police force came to investigate. When I felt a bit better we tried to extricate the jeep, but it was quite impossible. Its front wheels were in the bottom of the ditch and its rear wheels in the air. So we had a three-mile walk home; Harold had to confide his troubles to his tractor driver and get up before dawn with a tow rope; and I carry the scar on my forehead to remind me of one of the rabbits that got away.

The most unlikely visitor who ever came with us on one of these expeditions was the local parson. My father had been recounting some of our more reputable exploits—we did not tell him about the others—and I suppose he had made them seem rather fun. So next time I went home he said the vicar wanted to come, and would we take him. It was a particularly cold night in February, so we put the vicar in the front seat while I sat in the back with Dinah. So that I could get an uninterrupted view to 'spot' the rabbits, the windscreen was folded flat, and gusts of sleet froze on our foreheads so that we could chip the ice off in slivers.

As it happened we had some very good, more or less legitimate, sport. Indeed we had even gone to the extent of telling some of our neighbours we might come, because we thought the publicity of being caught poaching might not do the clergy any good. We made up for it by the excitements of the chase. Dinah excelled herself and so did Harold. No twisting and turning by a rabbit was violent enough to dislodge our spotlight, although some of the turns and lurches we executed in the process really did seem mechanically impossible. A winding stream divided one field and was, of course, no great obstacle to dog or rabbit, which would jump it. There were little bridges, with no sides, constructed of railway sleepers, quite wide and safe enough to take the jeep when going at right-angles to the brook-course. But going at right-angles would have entailed swinging the headlights off the rabbit, allowing its certain escape in darkness. So Harold took two of these bridges diagonally. Both times a ducking at speed seemed unavoidable, both times one wheel did go over the edge, and both times we were going fast enough to bounce back on to our level course again. It did not worry me, because I had grounds for belief that rolling out was by no means always fatal. The

136

vicar, on the other hand, had no such comforting philosophy. He had had a distinguished war career, but I gather he never prayed harder. And he had enough practice mixed with his theory to refuse all invitations to risk tempting providence twice.

7. Long Dogs

By the time Dinah had become expert on rabbits, myxomatosis had arrived—and rabbits went. For the next year or so it seemed that there would never again be sport to be had with rabbits. As my experience with dogs had grown, I had begun to hanker after a real, traditional lurcher, bred by gypsies; a lurcher capable of catching hares fairly on their own ground better than a pure-bred greyhound could.

To appreciate the qualities of a lurcher, it is necessary to understand just what is wanted from a thoroughbred greyhound.

Greyhounds have been bred for many centuries for coursing hares. Indeed the Egyptians are known to have used dogs almost indistinguishable from modern greyhounds, and there are good grounds for believing the breed to be the oldest and purest in the canine world. Of recent years greyhounds have also been used for dog racing, on tracks which provide a stuffed hare propelled by electricity as the 'quarry', but that is a business built entirely round betting and mere prostitution compared with a greyhound's natural function.

The purpose of coursing hares is not so much to catch the hare as to compare the qualities of the greyhounds which are competing. Two greyhounds at a time are put into slips, which consist of a pair of collars connected to the same lead. A handle protrudes from the top of this lead, and when it is pulled both collars fly open simultaneously. When the slipper, who is the man in charge of the dogs until they are free to run, judges that the instant has arrived to loose them after the hare, all he has to do is to pull the handle of his slip and both dogs are able to go at exactly the same instant.

The hares can be walked-up by a line of beaters, and either they are driven past the slipper or the slipper walks with his dogs with the beaters, waiting for a hare to start in front of him. In each case he holds the dogs until the hare has 'fair law', which is a start of about eighty to a hundred yards. He makes sure that both dogs can see their quarry and are straining at the leash—and then he slips them. The skill of the slipper can make or mar the course, because if he slips the hounds too soon the hare may not have a sporting chance and be 'chopped' before she gets into her stride. If he slips them too late they may have spent most of their initial zest before getting to terms.

The dog which catches the hare is not necessarily the winner. The winner is the dog which contributes most to the hare's downfall, and he is judged with an award of points for each effective move he makes, so that the victor can be decided just as easily if the hare escapes as if she is killed. At most coursing meetings many more hares get away than are caught. The hare knows where she is trying to get for safety, usually the cover of a field of roots or a wood or a hedge, through which she can weave to give the dogs the slip. In organized coursing meetings, like the Waterloo Cup, artificial cover is provided in the form of rushy banks, in which large drain-pipes are put. All the hares from the fields around are attracted to this area by feeding with oats or roots or carrots, so that every hare in the district knows where safety lies. When beaters walk them up from their forms and a pair of greyhounds is slipped after one of them, the hare's immediate reaction is to try to gain complete safety by taking refuge in a drain-pipe or in the thick cover provided for the purpose.

The fastest dog out of slips catches up with the hare first, and just as he is about to grab her, she will turn out of his path. Greyhounds are much more fleet than hares, and would catch any hare that continued to run in a straight line. But hares have a quite remarkable ability for turning and doubling in their tracks, allowing their pursuers to pass harmlessly by, perhaps within inches, and to overshoot by several yards, allowing the hare to turn again and make valuable ground towards the sanctuary she has chosen, before her pursuers can gather themselves and catch up, and force her to turn off course again.

A judge on horseback watches the whole course, and awards points to each dog as it outstrips its rival or forces the hare to deviate from the path she is trying to run. Whether the hare finally escapes—which is more often than not—or is caught, the judge indicates which hound he considers to have done the most effective work, and names him the winner.

A dog can win a course even though the hare has escaped unscathed, or he can lose a course in spite of catching her, if his opponent has run up a score of points for turning his quarry, only to find that the supreme reward has eluded him. The winner could be a complete fool, whose one virtue was speed, for he might have gone up time after time, only to be dodged at the last split second by the evasive hare. Furthermore, when a greyhound has had enough experience, he often begins to 'run cunning'. That is to say he does not try as hard as he might. He goes up to his hare, but instead of diving at her, and finding she has dodged him at the last moment and is yards away, he waits for his rival to turn her to him or for her to make the one fatal mistake necessary for him to take the chance of picking her up. Dogs that run cunning—or 'lurch'—like this are quite useless for coursing, because though they can catch hares all right, they do not pile up the necessary scoring points. For this reason coursing greyhounds see comparatively few hares in their working lives. They don't begin to course until about fifteen or eighteen months old, when they see just enough hares for them to discover that they are something they are allowed to kill and for which they will not be chastised, as they have been for poultry or for chasing or harrying stock. Then, when they are really keen, about the only other hares they see are those they encounter when they are running in trials or competitions. By this careful rationing it is possible to keep them for several seasons, before they learn that there is most chance of catching hares if they do not go up so fast that they over-run them. When that happens, or when the edge wears off their speed, they have to be retired, usually at about five or six years old, when the cream are kept for stud and most of the rest are put down.

Coursing is a most spectacular and sporting sport, not only because a very high proportion of hares escape, but because the course is over, one way or the other, so very quickly. Beagling is a war of attrition by comparison, and the hare is literally run to a standstill, being too exhausted at the last to outrun even the short-legged little hounds. In coursing the hare is either captured or escapes so soon that there are not many seconds for her to be frightened, and even a long course is so packed with action that there can be little time for reflection. The main reason that I have never kept coursing greyhounds is that their span of active life is so short. A dog that does not start work until about eighteen months old and is finished by about six is no good to me. When I have a dog, I reckon to find her a home for the rest of her span of life, and I have found lurchers to be the ideal solution.

A lurcher is not a mongrel but a deliberate cross-bred, the traditional breed of gypsies, who want dogs more for pot-boilers than for sport. Pure greyhound blood is diluted by crossing with a breed, to make up for some of the deficiencies of greyhounds, and the outcross used varies with district or personal choice. Traditionally sheepdog is the cross. The progeny have longer coats, more stamina and more brains than greyhounds. In Norfolk, a notable area for good lurchers, they still use 'Smithfields'—or Norfolk Lurchers. The old cattle dogs used to herd the fat cattle to Smithfield were lanky, long-coated dogs about the build of Bobtailed or Old English Sheepdogs. They had brains and stamina, and weather-resistant coats. The first cross was often not fast enough to come up with a hare which had had a good start, though they might be able to wear her down if the course could be prolonged without her taking cover. Ideally the lurcher should have three-quarters pure greyhound blood, procured either by mating a half-bred dog back to a thorough-bred bitch, or, less often, by mating two lurchers, each three-quarter bred. This was the less common practice.

Other outcrosses besides Smithfield sheepdogs were popular. Deerhound makes a wonderful cross, having good nose, superb eyesight, tough coat and temperament to match. Some people prefer greyhound-retriever cross. They used flat or curly coated retrievers, as Labradors would be too slow. On the Welsh Borders working sheepdog was popular, though not really big enough; Bedlington was sometimes used, though better as a cross with whippets for rabbiting; and since Saluki has become popular for legitimate coursing, it is not uncommon to find Saluki-lurchers. My objection to Salukis, which are supposed to have immense staying power, is that I have seen several that only gallop instead of really try. Anything can 'stay' if it is never really extended.

When there were plenty of rabbits about every gypsy worth the name had a lurcher or two. They caught rabbits and hares for the good of the table and most of them cost nothing whatever to keep. They lived off the land, killing rabbits for themselves and stealing whatever they could. Any dog which did neither was not worth his keep anyway.

In the Midlands there are very few true, Romany gypsies. There are hoards of 'scrap tatters', touring a restricted circuit with lorries, buying scrap, old motor tyres, copper wire and so on, returning at night to their caravan or to a cottage with a jumble of junk in the field behind it. Most of them like a 'long dog', but those with vans, 'the travellers', often buy them from one or two of their brethren, who are settled in a house with a yard behind. These are often the 'middle men' of the trade, the people who buy the scrap from the tatters and sort it. They burn the insulation off copper wire and have a certain amount of capital equipment, such as wire-bundling machinery, to sell their ware in bulk when they have sorted it.

These are the fellows to contact if you want a good lurcher. Many of them are smooth-tongued, plausible rogues, who will sell you rubbish if they can: so believe nothing but the evidence of your eyes. They are always buying and selling dogs from the gypsies and the travellers, and good ones and bad ones pass through their hands. Most of them love sport and keep the very best for themselves, and they will match them to kill more hares than their rivals for astonishingly large sums of money. I suppose that a high proportion of their income is strictly cash, which the taxman never hears about, and their needs extend little beyond food and beer, so that they have usually a wad of surplus pound notes, and no very fixed standard to evaluate them. Anyhow, it is by no means uncommon to see two scruffy ragamuffins match their dogs to kill the best of five or seven hares for £50 or £100 aside. And the money is peeled off a greasy bundle of fivers as if it was the price of a packet of Woodbines. For this reason, a dog that is outstanding is worth his weight in gold. They will think nothing of offering £20 or £30 on sight for a useful-looking dog, or trying to swap a lorry or a car for him. And if you won't sell, take care they don't steal him.

With such values, it is obviously almost impossible to buy a good 'made' dog. Furthermore, many of them run their dogs so hard that a good many get strained hearts early in life, and will not be much good anyway. The only chance for an outsider to get a good adult dog is to buy one that 'opens up'.

'Opening' is the supreme crime of lurchers. It simply means that they give tongue, or open up, under certain conditions, usually when their quarry starts to leave them and get away. Since most of the tatters' sport is by no means with the land-owner's permission, a dog that opens up is likely to get him-self shot by the keeper, and his owner pinched for poaching. If you intend using a lurcher on land where you have the right to go, one that gives tongue may be no disadvantage, and his price should be shillings, not pounds.

Gypsy was the first true lurcher I ever had, and I have never yet had a better. I got her as a pup of five weeks from a traveller who had had her parents for some years, so that I knew they were all right. The dog was a big, broken-haired half-bred deerhound called Peter, and the dam was a thoroughbred coursing—or ex-coursing—greyhound. Her satin skin was scarred and cross-scarred with barbed wire jags, and if they 'don't know what wire is', it is a fair bet that they have not had much work, except perhaps at legiti-mate coursing. I knew of Peter's reputation from a number of the local dog men, and both he and the bitch were stolen soon after I bought Gypsy. This was a much more reliable indication of their worth than any Kennel Club pedigrees could have been, because nobody takes the risk of stealing a lurcher unless he is sure it is a good one. The penalty of dis-covery is not prosecution, for the previous owner quite likely stole it too. The thief would get a real thumping with fists, feet and the nearest lump of cast-iron if he were caught.

So I knew Gypsy was bred all right. It remained to be seen how she would turn out. Nothing is more difficult to decide than the best of a litter of lurcher pups. From the very fact that they have both greyhound and collie or deerhound so closely in their blood, it is a fair assumption that some will revert to greyhound and be 'smooth lurchers', others to deer-hound or collie and be too cloddy to be fast, while a small percentage will have all the qualities you could desire. Even with pups bred from the lurchers on both sides, there are an enormous number of throwbacks.

The snag, with lurcher pups, is that they refuse to grow up uniformly. At six weeks old it is often impossible to be certain even if they will have broken (or rough) coats. At that stage they will have blunt muzzles, and if their limbs are fine and long, it is a fair assumption that they will be too fine when they mature, and end up virtually pure greyhound. If they seem to have plenty of bone, beware they are not the stocky sort, too slow to catch a cold.

Gypsy took ages to grow. She was only twenty-three inches at the shoulder at ten months old and looked like rather a rough, pipy whippet. Her coat was getting harsh and wiry and she went on growing after most breeds would have stopped, finishing up at twenty-four inches and forty-two pounds. Mandy, my present young bitch, is an inch and a half taller at the back than the front, like a kangaroo, though I am sure she will turn out all right because of her breeding, and even more because of the evidence of my fingers. She has great lumps of bone in her front legs, like the callous that forms after a fracture, and all that will go down and be absorbed as her front legs eventually grow longer and catch up the back as she grows older. A month ago she was so broad across the ribs that I was certain she would be one of the stiff and cloddy sort; now she has grown so much that she looks like a drain-pipe on unequal stilts. At no time in her life would I have bought her because she showed promise of being a good-looker. Yet it was the same with Gypsy when she was a pup, and she eventually developed into everything a good running dog should be.

So, if you buy a pup that is bred right, you have as much chance as the next man that he will turn out all right. It is the most difficult thing I know to buy a good grown dog. If you do manage to get a good one, keep it quiet or keep him under lock and key. I run an Alsatian in the compound, by the best police dog in the county; and when she rumbles threats to strangers, it is not bluff. She limits the danger of pilfering.

By the time Gypsy was four months old she was coming out with Dinah after rabbits. We had not then had myxomatosis in our district, and she took to rabbiting like a ferret to rats. As luck would have it, the foul disease struck just as she was about six months old, and for the next critical couple of months there were scores of rabbits about in varying stages of *extremis*. I have always marvelled how fast a rabbit can run when he is apparently almost blinded by the stinking pus that is killing him. Foul though it was, she got more experience and more confidence in that two months than she might otherwise have had in her first two seasons.

Greyhound men don't break their dogs in to hares until they are ready to course, at around eighteen months, largely so that they don't learn the tricks of the trade and run cunning. You cannot break a lurcher in too soon. I start at about four months and let them run everything they see until they get too keen and the danger arises that they will be hard run and strain themselves. Then I put them on a slip and do not let them go until the older dogs have tired their hare, when I let the fresh young dog slip in and catch her. It is such a powerful boost to her morale, not only to taste blood she has caught herself, but, flushed with success, to imagine she has beaten the older dogs. It is essential to have a good dog or so out as well, because young dogs are quite intelligent enough to take it easy and not try if experience teaches them they are not fast enough to catch the hare. They must get enough running to grow keen, be in at enough kills to appreciate the sweets of victory, but not be run hard enough to do any damage until they are mature.

If it is not possible to take them out with another dog, let them have a few gallops in small fields, where they will get unsighted long before they get tired. And try and run them first in July or August, when there are plenty of leverets about. Never run in the heat of the day but try and get out early, very early, in the morning. It will be cool to run, the dew will still be on the grass and the hares will be replete from a night's feeding. Hares do not run any better with a bellyful than dogs do. By this token, never run a dog less than six or eight hours after a meal. If I am expecting any hard courses, I feed my dogs at the same time the day before, to give them a good twenty-four hours to digest it. They can have a raw egg before they go out, but nothing more substantial. Their staple diet is as much meat as it takes to keep them fit and hard, with hard-baked bread to fill in the crevices.

I was lucky with Gypsy. I had no other dog to run with her, except my little whippet lurcher Dinah, who was wonderful at finding hares but not fast enough to overhaul them in a fair course. Gypsy was born in July and spent her first winter after rabbits, so easily that she had no doubts about her ability to catch anything that got up in front of her. I cannot over-emphasize the importance of this with a highly intelligent dog like a lurcher. It is not that she is a defeatist, but if she finds her quarry much faster in the first few runs she has, she is realistic enough to come to the conclusion it just isn't worth spending herself on a fool's errand. When she has once tasted blood and found the project practicable, she is game enough to go on trying for the rest of her life.

By the time she was just a year old the hay was cut and there were leverets about, bigger than good rabbits. We used to slip out soon after dawn for a walk across the meadows and newly cleared hay and clover fields. Dinah would hunt, nose well down, until she found where a hare had been feeding, and she would hunt his drag with the patience and accuracy of a beagle, until she put him up. She didn't do this many times before Gypsy could read the signs. She would work very well herself, but still keep her north eye on the older bitch. The instant she sensed Dinah was on to something her head would go up, and she was loping across the field in the same direction, on a converging line. It was a characteristic which distinguished her from pure greyhound, which is a gazehound and will keep its head up by instinct, ready to see the slightest movement. Given time, when they have learned to run cunning, greyhounds, or some greyhounds at least, will learn to hunt by scent. But it is considered a fault for any greyhound to 'get its head down'. Lurchers, on the other hand, should hunt by scent and by sight, and Gypsy was always prepared to try with her nose, but to leave a trail when she concluded Dinah was getting warm. The strong hares we put up those first summer mornings were either too good, and quickly got into roots or corn and escaped into concealment, or they were immature leverets.

It is not a mug's game, catching leverets. They are not as fast as a hare, nor do they run as far, sticking to their more restricted territory. But nothing can twist and turn and double like a leveret about three-quarters grown. A dog really has to get down to it, and a fast fool will go over and over and over his quarry, until he eventually lets it slip almost literally through his fangs into the nearest cover. Gypsy had killed quite enough rabbits to have confidence in her ability, but she was very puzzled by her first few hares. Then she found the knack, and by October was ready to take on all comers, and gave wonderful sport.

The one snag with running lurchers is the risk of accident. I met my present vet after Gypsy had 'pulled' a back claw. Stupidly, I had let her run on rather hard ground after a catch of frost. She had a longish course and I noticed blood on her foot when she returned. The claw had been torn off leaving a stump of 'quick', which was naturally very painful and made her go lame next day. I had recently moved, and was twenty miles from the vet I had known for years; so I took her to a local vet. He told me that it would never do any good and that he would take it off. It was fairly near the end of her first season, so I said that I was not much in favour of having a running dog's toe off, because of the additional strain on the ones that were left, and I would give her a few weeks to recover. Then, if it was still no better—and he insisted it would not be—I would bring her again. Meanwhile I went to the Waterloo Cup and asked one of the best trainers if his greyhounds ever pulled a claw.

'Often,' he said, 'they aren't trying if they don't.'

I asked him what he did about it and he said he rested them three weeks. So I told him I had been advised to have my bitch's toe off.

'Who the hell by?' he asked. I told him. 'He's only a "hoss-and-cow man", I should think,' he said. 'Never take a running dog to a "hoss-and-cow man".'

I never had better advice. I rang the local greyhound track and asked for the address of their vet—who happens to be a good 'hoss-and-cow man' too—and I give the other sort a very wide berth indeed. It is an unfortunate thing that lurchers are pretty accident prone. You cannot gallop cross-country at forty miles an hour after a twisting, weaving, dodging hare without making accidental contact with all sorts of things. And, at that speed, something has to suffer.

Barbed wire is easily the worst culprit, and Gypsy averaged about forty stitches a season in her first three years. My vet was as tolerant as he is sporting, and put up with frequent interruptions to his Sunday dinner with the greatest good humour. We always went coursing on Sunday morning, and I felt rather self-conscious about the time I was forced to go; so I bought a do-it-yourself kit, and now I stitch up all the simple ones myself. But it is quite imperative to get professional help for any belly wounds or wounds under the 'armpit' or in the groin. It is not uncommon for wounds here to suck in air when the limb articulates, and 'blow up' the skin in the area. Amber, a four-year-old bitch, hit a stump this spring, when she was close to her hare going through a very open hedge. She dislocated her hip, and had to be destroyed. But that is the only really serious accident any of my dogs have suffered. Aerodromes are the most hazardous places to course, as the hare often chooses to run straight up a runway.

This almost inevitably wears off the 'stoppers', the little pads on the inside of the dog's front legs; but last season, when Gypsy had a longish course up a runway, she apparently 'pulled' a back claw, and then wore away first the quick and then the whole of the first knuckle bone. It not only stopped her coursing for six weeks, but still opens up if she has a run over particularly hard or stony ground.

Nevertheless, accidents only stand out in the memory because they are exceptional. Old Gypsy has killed me several hundred hares, including the memorable day she killed four against nil of the pure greyhound she was running against. But it is not only the dogs that take the risks.

I had been invited to have a day's coursing with a farmer, and naturally imagined we were going to run on his farm. We were joined by half a dozen of the scrap tatting fraternity, each with a dog, and we set out into the fields. Sport was very good, and we eventually arrived in the middle of a sixty-acre field. I was walking next to my host, who casually remarked:

'If you see a bloke in a Land-Rover, run like hell, he'll shoot.'

I had been brought up to believe that, if you must go poaching, the proper time was at dusk or just as it was getting light. In exceptional cases, and if the habits of the landowner were stereotyped enough, it might be permissible to venture out on wet Sunday afternoons or while he was at morning service. Yet here was I quite innocently accompanying as rough a gang of blackguards as I could conceive, in broad daylight on Saturday afternoon, on land apparently owned by a gentleman with homicidal tendencies. Never has a field looked so large nor sheltering hedges so far off.

Gypsy, of course, was in her element. She had been bred to live off the land and thieving came as naturally to her as chasing hares. If she caught a rabbit about the place at home, and I was too busy to take it from her at once, she would start to eat it. Within ten minutes it would be gone, fur, feet, head, the lot; and there she would sit, as blandly bloated as a tycoon after an expense account meal. Her table manners left something to be desired, too. We were sitting round the fire eating afternoon tea from little tables and making polite conversation with a somewhat starchy guest. Gypsy lay by the fire and then moved because she got too hot. She timed her journey so that she passed the guest's table as he turned his head to speak. Without faltering in her stride, she nicked the sandwich from his plate as smoothly as a conjurer. He never even noticed, so I offered him another. Three minutes later she had that, and, his hands groping for it as he talked, a slightly puzzled expression did flit across his face. He appeared worried that he was getting absent-minded, so I passed him the plate and he took another without a word. Even then, with his suspicions half aroused, she took the third without actually getting caught; but it made me laugh and it gave the game away.

I have seen the old bitch lie by the kitchen fire as innocent as a cherub, and if someone goes to the pantry door she will simply cock an ear. It has a drop latch, and if it does not click home she knows in an instant. But she will not move a muscle. She will wait until she thinks nobody is watching, then she will sneak off, shove the door open with her nose, pinch anything available—from a joint of meat to a bit of dry bread—and be back on the hearth in a few seconds. If there is nobody about she will gulp down the spoil as if she was never fed. But if she is disturbed she will put it down and lie on it, in dewy-eyed innocence, until the coast is clear again. That is intelligent private enterprise.

She is a good house-dog, a vicious guard if necessary, tough and selfish with the other dogs, unflinchingly faithful to me; and the one thing she prefers to food is sport. Anybody is welcome to showdogs, for me, however expensive and effete. I like a dog whose prowess and brains and guts command respect.

Some might despise my dogs because they are 'no better than mongrels', but a mongrel is the product of chance, and my dogs have been produced by carefully mixing the blood of different breeds for a specific purpose. Indeed, Mandy, my youngest lurcher, just beginning to 'run clever' at eighteen months, is the rather unusual product of a lurcher to lurcher mating. Her ancestors, on both sides, were originally produced by crossing pure coursing greyhound to half-bred greyhound-cattle dog. These were the Smithfields of East Anglia which drove cattle fed on the grazing lands of Norfolk to London for slaughter. A few gypsies have jealously guarded these strains of lurcher until they eventually bred true. Although no Canine Society recognizes them, they are as blue-blooded as their owners, who do not need the records of Somerset House to establish their superiority over aristocratic Gorgios, incapable of living off the land.

Working sheepdogs, the fleet, brainy dogs which enliven agricultural shows by their displays of crafty patience, are as carefully bred as any showdog, though the exhibition world does not recognize their pedigrees. Most winning gundogs at Field Trials, chosen for stamina and brains and courage, would stand as little chance of an award, in the show ring, as a show greyhound would of winning the Waterloo Cup.

My one pedigree bitch, Tough, is an Alsatian. She would stand no chance of winning in the show ring, but she is bred from an impressive line of Police Dogs, with a formidable array of arrests to their credit. She is as game and brainy as her parents, and once I have made her understand what it is that I want, her single purpose is to comply. She will attack on command or treat strangers with dignified hospitality, according to my wish. Generations of her breeding have shone in the circles where deeds rate higher than looks, and, though she might not win any prizes, I can leave my wife in an isolated house, in the certain knowledge that it would be a foolhardy intruder who entered uninvited.

I would not give a 'Thank You' for some of the prize-winning fox terriers, as useless down a fox earth as a pampered Peke, or the setters and Airedales which win only because they have clever handlers to kneel reverently on one knee, holding head and tail in the exact postures which will delight the judge's eye. The things that matter to me are that my dogs have brains and health, and that their temperament makes them good companions. I love working dogs, whether they are sheepdogs or hounds, gundogs or lurchers, and I don't mind how obscure their pedigree is or if they were rescued from the nearest home for lost dogs.